Government Information Management

Other Titles in This Series

Marketing Scientific and Technical Information, edited by William R. King and Gerald Zaltman

Information Services: Economics, Management, and Technology, edited by Robert M. Mason and John E. Creps

Westview Special Studies in Information Management

Government Information Management:
A Counter-Report of the Commission on Federal Paperwork
Elliott R. Morss and Robert F. Rich

In this timely critique of federal procedures, the authors identify the underlying causes of the current overload of information/paperwork in government and explain why the problem cannot be controlled until the causes are eliminated or neutralized. Using a calculus they have developed for estimating the "value" and "burden" of federal information, the authors argue that information should be considered essential only to the degree that it can increase citizen well-being. How often a certain piece of information gets used has little or no bearing on its actual value. Recommendations are made for using comparative studies of information practices to direct reform in regulatory agencies, for improving evaluation procedures, and for putting information collection on a compensatory basis as an incentive for reducing excesses.

Elliott R. Morss, director of research for Development Alternatives, Inc., served as study director for the Commission on Federal Paperwork. Robert F. Rich, assistant professor of politics and public affairs at the Woodrow Wilson School of Public and International Affairs at Princeton University, previously was research scientist–project director at the Institute for Social Research, Center for Research on the Utilization of Scientific Knowledge, University of Michigan.

Government Information Management: A Counter-Report of the Commission on Federal Paperwork

Elliott R. Morss
and Robert F. Rich

with the assistance of
Thomas Grooms and Victoria Sorsby

Westview Press / Boulder, Colorado

Westview Special Studies in Information Management

Published in 1980 in the United States of America by
  Westview Press, Inc.
  5500 Central Avenue
  Boulder, Colorado 80301
  Frederick A. Praeger, Publisher

Library of Congress Cataloging in Publication Data
Morss, Elliott R.
  Government information management.
  (Westview special studies in information management)
  Bibliography: p.
  Includes index.
  1. Government paperwork–United States. I. Rich, Robert F., joint author. II. United States Commission on Federal Paperwork. III. Title. IV. Series.
JK468.P34M67   353.0071'4   79-27064
ISBN: 0-89158-596-6

Printed and bound in the United States of America

Contents

Tables

Abbreviations

ADP	automated data processing
ANSI	American National Standards Institute
CAB	Civil Aeronautics Board
CPSC	Consumer Product Safety Commission
CSC	Civil Service Commission
DAWN	Drug Alert Warning Network
DBMS	data base management system
EDP	electronic data processing
EPA	Environmental Protection Agency
FCC	Federal Communications Commission
FDA	Food and Drug Administration
FMC	Federal Maritime Commission
FTC	Federal Trade Commission
GAO	General Accounting Office
GNP	gross national product
HEW	Department of Health, Education, and Welfare
ICC	Interstate Commerce Commisson
IRS	Internal Revenue Service
MIS	management information system
NEISS	National Electronic Injury Surveillance System
NRC	Nuclear Regulatory Commission
OEO	Office of Economic Opportunity
OMB	Office of Management and Budget
OSHA	Occupational Safety and Health Administration
SEC	Securities and Exchange Commission
SSA	Social Security Administration
VA	Veterans Administration

Preface

In 1974, Congress established the Commission on Federal Paper-work. Its mandate was to report to Congress and the president its findings and recommendations on how to minimize the information-reporting burden within the public sector and yet ensure that the federal government would have the information necessary to fulfill its responsibilities. Before its final report was issued and it closed down almost three years later, the commission had spent about $9 million, or more than twice as much as any previous federal commission.

A counter-report should not have been necessary. However, we strongly believe that the commission's final report does not reflect the hard work of the commission. In essence, we feel that the report fails to provide direction for future government information management efforts. The report does not identify and come to grips with the primary causes for the excessive amount of paperwork generated; instead, the report lists the commission's "successes" and makes only narrow recommendations for future actions.

This preface details the commission's failures and the reasons for them, and the remainder of the counter-report constitutes our view of what the commission's report should have been. So the reader may fully understand what we are advocating, detailed examples are offered. Also, recommendations are made for those areas in which further work is required if the proposed concepts are to become operational.

Finally, the significance of the volume's title should be mentioned. This work is a counter-report *of* rather than *to* the commission because both authors worked for the commission, Dr. Morss as director of a study group and Professor Rich as a consultant to him.

What are the different approaches the commission could have followed? First, it could have played ombudsman, i.e., followed up on complaints from the public and attempted to correct abuses; second, it could have examined information practices on an agency-by-agency basis and recommended that unnecessary actions be terminated; and third, it could have attempted to identify and recommend steps to eliminate the underlying factors that lead the federal government to ask the public for excessive—and sometimes nonessential—information. A strong, albeit cynical, argument could have been made for focusing on the first two strategies: since the underlying factors are as intractable as death and taxes, a commission might as well do as much "weed cutting" as possible (cf. Herbert Kaufman, *Red Tape: Its Origins, Uses, and Abuses* [Washington, D.C.: Brookings Institution, 1977]). But the implications of focusing on only those two strategies are that weeds tend to grow up again and, therefore, new commissions with similar mandates would have to be established periodically.

Although we have some sympathy for the argument concerning the intractability of the underlying factors, we feel it should be subjected to an empirical test. In fact, we believe that the underlying factors should be identified and efforts should be made to formulate techniques that government officials could use to eliminate asking for excessive information.

Although we do not believe the commissioners were ever presented with these options, the commission's total resources were adequate to carry out all three strategies. Even though far more resources were allocated to achieving results by following the first two strategies, there were sufficient resources allocated to the third to realize significant results there as well, and this book will offer evidence that considerable resources were indeed devoted to the third strategy.

Although one can hypothesize that the problems of excessive government information are intractable, it, regrettably, is still only a hypothesis; despite a $9 million outlay, the commission's efforts did not test the hypothesis. The commission did not make a sincere effort to deal with either the immediate or the underlying reasons for federal excesses. To understand why the commission's efforts were primarily a waste of the taxpayers' money, it is necessary to know something about the commissioners and the commission's staff.

If one wanted to find ways to eliminate crime, one would not establish a study panel dominated by criminals. And yet, in a very real sense, this is exactly what happened in the case of the Commission on Federal Paperwork. Among the commissioners, there were four congressmen, the director of the Office of Management and Budget (OMB), the director of the Internal Revenue Service (IRS), the comptroller general, and, later, the secretary of Health, Education, and Welfare (HEW). Although the other commissioners had some conception of the national interest in mind, they were not in a position to overrule these powerful federal officials. The results were as one might expect.

By proposing excessively general legislative mandates and by requesting a great deal of irrelevant information from the executive branch, Congress is one of the primary information/paperwork offenders. Yet nowhere in the commission's report or in its detailed studies are these points even addressed. It is inexcusable that such an obvious case for attention is ignored. It is understandable, however, when one considers the commission's large congressional representation.

The Internal Revenue Service probably imposes a greater burden on respondents, both individual and corporate, than any other federal entity. We use the term "probably" because Donald Alexander, director of the IRS at the time and a commissioner, flatly refused to allow the commission to study the IRS's respondent burden. Other commissioners could have forced the issue but chose not to, probably in hopes of gaining Alexander's cooperation on other issues.

While the comptroller general appeared to assume the role of a "neutral observer," the Office of Management and Budget took a very active interest in the work of the commission. Personnel from the OMB attended all commission meetings open to them, and often as many as three staff members attended. By keeping abreast of the commission's activities, the OMB was able to keep the commission staff from carrying out activities that would cause the OMB to look bad. For example, the OMB demanded and received from federal departments and agencies reports on what was being done to comply with the presidential directive to reduce paperwork. When commission staff members requested the reports, the response was, "They are being printed." Of course, this was far from the truth. Information is power, and the OMB did not want to cede any of its power to the commission.

The commission spent a considerable amount of time and re-sources examining the paperwork problems of the Department of Health, Education, and Welfare. The secretary of HEW did not become a commissioner until most of the HEW reports had been completed. In short, the commission treaded lightly when commis-sioners' interests were involved. Unfortunately for the commission and the American taxpayer, the commissioners were interested in protecting those organizations that were the most flagrant paper-work violators.

In theory, if the senior staff of a commission has integrity and pro-fessional expertise, that staff can do a lot to keep the commissioners "on track." The senior staff of the paperwork commission had neither. The first director was fired, and of the three congressional aides then hired to fill the three top management slots, none had technical competence in the information management field and each was dependent on a particular political constituency.

Even under those circumstances, the situation need not have been hopeless. The commission had adequate funds to attract a profes-sional staff, and indeed some very competent individuals were re-cruited to fill staff positions and to act as consultants. Regrettably, their work was not used effectively. Instead of soliciting their advice on how to tackle particular issues, the senior staff would devise a plan of action and then order the staff to implement it. For example, it was decided to collect from corporations and private businesses data on the costs of complying with federal information requests. The data were collected, but the professional staff was disbanded before it had the time to do a thorough analysis of the data. Because of the absence of senior staff–technical staff coordination, the com-mission did what it was created to prevent – namely, it requested in-formation from the public and made little use of it.

It should be clear that the cards were stacked against the commis-sion's producing specific techniques that could be experimented with. However, it is our conviction that valuable work was done by the commission staff, and we do not want to see it wasted. Indeed, the following chapters should be seen as an attempt to salvage some-thing useful out of the $9 million expenditure of taxpayers' money.

Elliott R. Morss
Robert F. Rich

Acknowledgments

This book grew out of the work performed in conjunction with the Value/Burden Study Group of the Commission on Federal Paperwork. The work of that study group's staff contributed greatly to the analysis presented in this volume, and those staff members are to be thanked: Stephen Baratz, Richard Bullock, Gerald Calderone, Robert Eckert, Gayle Eisenstadt, Deborah Frucht, Thomas Grooms, and Valerie Mitchell. We are particularly grateful to Ann Macaluso for her continued support.

The study group also contracted for some research that was of help in completing this volume. In this regard, we want to thank Nathan Caplan, Dorothy Glancy, Donald King, Daniel Tunstall, and Harrison Wehner for their contributions.

We offer special thanks to Lucy Rich for help in editing several of the chapters, and finally, we thank Amy Kerlin of Princeton University for her tireless efforts in typing and proofreading our manuscript.

E.R.M.
R.F.R.

Government Information Management

1
Introduction

Our forefathers started us on a course that is information intensive from both a political and an economic standpoint. The separation of powers, checks and balances, the Bill of Rights with its due process clause, not to mention the federal administrative structure, necessitate a tremendous amount of paperwork. Checks and balances, along with the separation of powers, frequently require the executive branch, Congress, and the courts to simultaneously engage in similar information activities in the process of developing independent positions on the same issues. The Bill of Rights and its due process clause, designed to protect the rights of the individual and property, cause a considerable amount of paperwork in the attempt to ensure privacy and confidentiality.

Two dramatic changes occurred fairly recently that bear directly on our work. First, the information industry expanded after World War II on a scale that is difficult to comprehend. Information production and application activities now take up an increasingly significant part of our gross national product (GNP), and a recent National Academy of Sciences study found that the federal government invested $2 billion in fiscal year 1977 to acquire and use knowledge of social problems alone. This increased investment in information flow has made the customary methods of handling information inadequate. As a result, new systems of accessing and retrieving information have had to be devised to meet the user demands. The creation of these systems has been stimulated by rapid advances in computer hardware and software. In a sense, we have witnessed a case of computer capability creating its own information demands. Second, as social concerns other than economic growth have assumed importance, we have increasingly become a regulated society. Unfortunately the "regulation explosion" has also

1

increased information activities, and now steps must be taken to
alleviate the excessive paperwork created by these changes.

The Commission on Federal Paperwork was established in 1974
to eliminate excessive paperwork while ensuring that the information needed for good governance was available. Essentially the commission was given the tasks of (1) assessing the effectiveness of current federal information management practices, (2) identifying the
causes and roots of problems that were uncovered, and (3) making
recommendations for a more effective federal information management system.

Because of the greater investment in information resources, information managers have become increasingly important in the federal
government. For any particular agency, they are responsible for
establishing procedures governing the acquisition or procurement,
processing, dissemination, use, and application of information. People who hold these key positions are not formally (i.e., by title)
known as information managers. Sometimes they are special
assistants to a cabinet member, and sometimes they are part of a
special office for information policy. Whatever their title, their function is carried out in every government organization.

The effective information manager is one who ensures that the
necessary and *appropriate* information resources are available for purposes of problem solving and, at the same time, minimizes (or,
ideally, eliminates) unnecessary and inappropriate information.
There is an information overload problem in government, and public
officials put a high premium on receiving only relevant information,
efficiently and quickly. The critical task implicit in the paperwork
commission's charter was to find a way to distinguish between what
is relevant and what is irrelevant information.

In analyzing federal information management practices, we found
it particularly useful to think of the values and burdens of information. We mostly concentrated our efforts on assessing the values
and burdens of paperwork, emphasizing (a) the reporting requirements that the government imposes on itself and on institutions
external to the government, (b) the internal rules and regulations
that require paperwork, (c) the procedures for acquiring information
and other resources that require paperwork, and (d) the routine
reporting systems that generate paperwork on a regular basis. This
approach forced us to focus on the process of governance more than

on the substance of any particular policy or program. It also enabled us to evaluate the extent to which federal information practices were designed with some kind of implicit or explicit value/burden calculus in mind.

Given this background, we set out to uncover the values and burdens of information and paperwork in government. On the surface, finding instances in which burden exceeded value did not appear to be a difficult undertaking. The commission uncovered numerous cases of excessive paperwork that were "blatantly indefensible" in light of the burdens they imposed on the public and their irrelevance to federal government needs. However, the task proved to be far more difficult that it seemed. The "blatantly indefensible" cases constituted only a small portion of the totality of excessive federal paperwork/information practices. The bulk of the problems were less obvious and required a careful weighing of the value and burden of each information activity.

Another difficulty became apparent when we attempted to develop recommendations to deal with the problem. While the commission was active, attention could be brought to bear on specific instances of excessive paperwork. It was another matter, however, to come up with a set of recommendations that would lead to a permanent reduction in excessive paperwork/information practices. To be successful in this quest, we had to identify the root causes of the excesses and develop recommendations to counter or eliminate them. The commission will not have a long-term impact on the paperwork problem unless its recommendations focus on eliminating root causes. The analyses presented in the chapters that follow are designed to provide effective information management tools for dealing with the root causes of paperwork-intensive government activities.

Root Causes of Federal
Paperwork/Information Excesses

In completing our work for the commission, we came away with the strong feeling that "Type III" errors were being committed, i.e., the right solution to the wrong problem was being found. Aspirin was being administered when it was not clear whether the patient was prone to ulcers or whether he had used aspirin for so many years that he had become, therefore, immune to it.

With this in mind, we felt that it was essential to start with a framework for understanding federal information practices. If recommendations for long-term change are to be made, attention must be focused on the root causes of excessive paperwork. The following is all-inclusive in the sense that all excesses should be attributable to one or a combination of the causes listed.

1. Absence of national priorities
2. Bureaucratic dynamics
3. Political dynamics
4. Ability of government to avoid paying a large share of the economic and psychological costs of information collection
5. Lack of management tools that would permit government officials to assess the effectiveness of their information systems
6. The technician-user misfit, i.e., the inability or unwillingness of policymakers and social science researchers to define their information needs and the unwillingness of the information managers to take this attitude into account
7. Citizen distrust
8. Importance of being viewed as unimportant

1. *Absence of National Priorities*

Ideally the responsibilities of federal officials in all branches of government should be determined by a continuous effort to establish national goals, to decide upon priorities, and to develop plans to implement those priorities. Any implementation plan should be directed toward maximizing citizen well-being within the contexts of a given set of national priorities and the budget. An implementation plan should define individual and organizational responsibilities within the federal government so that each official in the government hierarchy can relate his or her day-to-day activities to the absolute standard of "success," realizing the national priorities and goals.

Failure to continually define priorities generates excessive paperwork/information activities for several reasons. First, not having determined precise objectives results in ambiguity, misunderstanding, redundancy, and, hence, inefficient management. Second, the absence of a hierarchical set of objectives and responsibilities makes it impossible to assess the value of any particular information activity in relation to other available information activities. More importantly from a management point of view, it is difficult to allocate scarce resources wisely when there is no specific set of objectives.

Unfortunately there is little recognition in government of the importance of determining priorities. The government does not engage in a systematic review of national priorities; instead, it usually only makes marginal changes in budgetary allocations. The practice of making marginal changes on a year-by-year basis has several unfortunate consequences: (1) systemic review rarely occurs; (2) heads of agencies and decision makers concentrate on maintaining their staffs, budgets, and programs irrespective of their value; and (3) implicit mutual accommodation agreements develop between the legislative and executive branches of government—e.g., "we will regularly increase your budget; in return, you will help us when we need it." The practice also results in high paperwork/information costs. Each federal agency, each department, and each subdivision determines its own operational objectives and information needs in an uncoordinated fashion. Frequently these determinations are made on a self-serving basis and require continuous information input to support the unit's existence.

A picture emerges of government officials working without any legitimate standards of success. How do they know what substantive goals they are supposed to be working toward? To whom are they accountable? Government cannot function without answers to these questions, and therefore paperwork-intensive answers, which can be derived by observing government practices, have been formulated. Officials are working toward the goal of maintaining their organization, and they are accountable to higher-level civil servants who are also concerned with maintaining the organization. As a result, citizen well-being, which could be specified if priorities were defined, is only given lip service.

In addition, a lack of clearly defined responsibilities sets the stage for competition among the various branches and agencies of the federal government as well as among the different levels of government. A certain amount of competition would appear desirable, but, for reasons to be discussed in the next two sections, the competition has led to excessive paperwork/information practices and inefficient management.

2. Bureaucratic Dynamics

Unfortunately government officials are not always motivated to work for the public good. Although the desired dynamic is

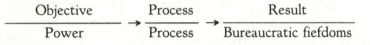

$$\frac{\text{Objective}}{\text{Citizen well-being}} \rightarrow \frac{\text{Process}}{\text{Process}} \rightarrow \frac{\text{Result}}{\text{Public benefit}}$$

What often develops is

$$\frac{\text{Objective}}{\text{Power}} \rightarrow \frac{\text{Process}}{\text{Process}} \rightarrow \frac{\text{Result}}{\text{Bureaucratic fiefdoms}}$$

and thus information becomes a vehicle for power, control, and bureaucratic growth and maintenance. Since information can only serve this function if access to it is limited, bureaucrats tend to jealously guard information as they consider it a vital tool to obtaining and maintaining power. Resource sharing and interagency cooperation are rare; when they do occur, it is often the result of a mandate.

Elaborate classifaction mechanisms have been established to limit information access. In addition, a 1975 commission study on confidentiality indicated that significant barriers to obtaining nonclassifiable information are raised through finding ingenious ways to delay the transfer of information. The bureaucratic reaction usually is to generate a new information base in order to maintain power rather than to focus directly on solving the problems associated with information transfer.

There are specific kinds of bureaucratic behavior associated with paperwork. Bureaucrats tend to guard or protect the ownership and control of information resources, and they resist sharing those resources so that a code of secrecy develops—secrecy that goes far beyond the boundaries that could be dictated by a concern for national security. There is an almost exclusive reliance on information resources generated in-house, and often a distrust of external resources; there is a lack of coordination of federal information management practices across agencies; and information is acquired, processed, and used to meet organizational ends as opposed to more substantive goals. What is needed by the organization on a day-to-day basis becomes the accepted bureaucratic criterion for action rather than good management and agency coordination.

3. Political Dynamics

The competitive factor also influences the information activities of politically appointed and elected officials. Unlike bureaucratic dynamics, the goal of political officials is not to use information to build and maintain bureaucratic "turf" but to use information to secure personal influence. Politics can be characterized as bargaining among individuals, and information is a valuable bartering commodity. Officials sometimes seek out information that casts them in a good light and occasionally attempt to undermine or suppress information that might make them look bad. Political dynamics are also related to the absence of a set of defined national priorities. The political executive cannot point to a set of objectives/standards toward which his program/agency is striving. Instead, he is forced into the position of making himself look good (i.e., image building). In this effort, information can be critical, and consequently, the potential for excesses is great.

Congress, in its endeavor to oversee the executive branch, often requires information that greatly exceeds any realistic appraisal of what is needed. Congress may not be sure what to evaluate so it asks for everything. In response, the executive branch develops information in the hope that it will protect the executive from anticipated legislative demands (there are numerous examples of the executive branch developing information resources in anticipation of congressional requests—information that was never used). At other times, Congress enacts legislation with objectives so vague that they result in many interpretations. This results in the collection of vast quantities of information because it is difficult to anticipate what Congress wants.

All of the practices described thus far result in information activities that are inappropriate because they do not lead directly to citizen well-being.

4. Ability of Government to Avoid Paying a Large Share of the Costs of Information Collection

Business, individuals, and lower-level governments are required to provide information to the federal government without compensation. The burden on respondents is substantial; it is estimated that the economic costs alone exceed $20 billion annually. Because the government does not have to bear the costs, there is reason to believe that federal officials make excessive demands for information since it appears to them to be a free commodity. The view that information is free is clearly an important cause of excessive paperwork/information activities.

5. Lack of Management Tools

If paperwork/information is to be effectively managed by the federal government, it is essential that techniques for control be developed and used, and methods to assess the value and burden (cost) of paperwork/information are especially important (see Chapter 4). Other techniques, such as the use of comparative analyses (see chapters 6–7), must also be developed and employed. Little has been done to date in these areas, and this serves as a barrier to the elimination of excessive paperwork.

6. The Technician-User Misfit

Today nearly half of the GNP and over half of all wages originate from the production, processing, and distribution of information goods and services.[1] Yet we continue to ignore the basic communications theory, which specifies that man uses information to acquire knowledge and understanding. We have established and continue to establish enormous and redundant information systems that are obsolete because the concept on which they are based is erroneous.

In current Western thought, information systems are based on the presupposition that knowledge–i.e., verified truth–is the end result of a linear process. This mistaken notion can be diagrammed as follows:

139 problems w/ MIS
in KJD sys

data →information →knowledge →"right" policy/decision

But it is a mistake to conceive of decision making in input/output terms. The problems of locating and tracing information/data as it flows through decision-making channels challenges the underlying assumption of those systems designers who believe in "technological fixes," the assumption that constructing and following a detailed process (flow) diagram leads to a more innovative and effective information system. If management/policy deliberations and decision processes do not follow a simple, logical continuum, then the relevance of the solutions offered are called into question. Indeed these so-called solutions may produce more paperwork and still not succeed in reducing the excesses.

Policies and decisions are not simply the result of data input. Even if they were, policymakers have difficulty distinguishing between relevant and "related to" information—the latter may be vast in quantity. Policymakers are also unable to anticipate their data needs, but the information technician is undaunted. What the policymaker cannot do, the technician will—supply data (even when the application is unclear). This, in a nutshell, is the information overload problem.

This problem

64

The consequences of this way of thinking are serious. Wrong and irrelevant data are often collected, and the use of computers is substituted for creative thinking and problem solving because of the mistaken assumption that computers will automatically produce the right decision. The technical system can only reflect the efficiency and accuracy of the management process. Today hardware and software systems exist that are far more sophisticated and complex than the situation warrants and/or the potential user can usefully apply.

7. Citizen Distrust

A case of excessive paperwork exists when the costs of collecting it include a psychological component—frustration, anger, hostility, distrust, etc. Citizens may question the necessity, relevance, and use of the information they are asked to supply, and the consequence of this distrust is an increased federal paperwork burden (cost) in relation to its value.

If a federal agency sends out a questionnaire and an insufficient number of forms are returned because of citizen distrust, the agency has three options: (1) drop the project, (2) proceed to make assumptions based on a limited sample, or (3) send out the questionnaire again, perhaps making its completion and return mandatory. If the government drops the project, then a burden exists in terms of wasted resources. The second option is ultimately inefficient from a management point of view, and option three will clearly produce yet more paperwork. Clearly, the cost of information and the amount of paperwork activity are greater when there is citizen distrust.

The concern over "trust" is documented by surveys that show a striking reduction in confidence in the nation's institutions. A Harris survey (see Table 1.1) is indicative of survey findings on the subject. There is now less confidence in the Congress and the executive branch of the federal government than in almost all other institutions covered in the Harris poll. In part, the general disillusionment is attributable to a more realistic citizen perspective than previously existed, and this may be partially due to the activities of the media and public interest groups. Nevertheless, even after allowing for a reasonable increase in the citizens' "sense of reality," it is obvious that a striking reduction in trust has occurred.

These findings suggest that even if the volume of federal information requests had not increased in recent years, the psychological burden associated with information collecting would have increased. If the trust in government has declined as rapidly as the survey data suggest, there is reason to believe that people will be "bothered even more" by the federal government requests for information, and this increase in the psychological burden suggests the likelihood of even greater paperwork/information excesses.

8. Importance of Being Viewed as Unimportant

The analyses presented above are sufficient to suggest that the federal government will continue to demand excessive amounts of information. Unfortunately, there is reason to believe that "excessive" may turn to "surfeit" because no federal official is likely to give a great deal of time to the elimination of excesses in his information system. In most cases, the difference in cost between the operation of existing information systems and their operation if excesses were removed is not great in relation to other cost changes that government officials can bring about. Quite simply from the perspec-

Table 1.1

Confidence in Institutions

As far as the people in charge of running (INSTITUTIONS) are concerned, would you say you have a great deal of confidence, only some confidence, or hardly any confidence at all in them?

	Percent saying "Great deal of confidence"							
	1966	1967	1971	1972	1973	1974	1975	1976
The Executive Branch of the Federal Government	41	39	23	27	19	28	13	11
Congress	42	42	19	21	29	18	13	9
U.S. Supreme Court	50	51	23	28	33	40	28	22
The Military	62	56	27	35	40	33	24	23
Medicine	72	66	61	48	57	50	43	42
Major Companies	55	57	27	27	29	21	19	16
Organized Labor	22	27	14	15	20	18	14	10
Higher Education	61	62	37	33	44	40	36	31
Organized Religion	41	41	27	30	36	32	24	24
The Press	29	27	18	18	30	25	26	20
Television News	25	21	22	17	41	31	35	28
The Scientific Community	56	46	32	37	--	--	--	--

Source: The Harris Survey. 1967 figures computed from January 1967 (n=1064) Harris poll. (1967 data are for adults who had voted in 1960, 1962, 1964, or 1966, or who were registered to vote.)

tive of a government official, the cost of checking for excesses is not worth the benefit that might result. Clearly there are dramatic exceptions to this rule, but most federal officials simply do not consider excessive paperwork an important problem.

Overview of Chapters in This Volume

Obviously all the root causes listed above are related to each other. We view the absence of national priorities and bureaucratic and political dynamics as the overarching causes. The others, also very important, follow from these three. The root causes represent the framework for our analysis of federal information management practices. The chapters in this book analyze some of the root causes in further detail, both conceptually and empirically, and provide some tools that can be used by officials concerned with more effective management.

Chapters 2 and 3 are devoted to providing a detailed analysis of what we consider to be the key to continued paperwork excesses in the public sector, the bureaucratic and political pathologies related to governance. Chapter 2 synthesizes what we know about bureaucratic dynamics and its relationship to paperwork burdens. It also describes individual symptoms of the overall problem. Chapter 3 describes and assesses various incentives that might be used to encourage public officials to adopt more effective information management practices.

In dealing with a number of the root causes of paperwork, the development and implementation of better information assessment techniques are essential. In Chapter 5 one such assessment technique, based on the value/burden approach, is presented. This method attempts to measure the value and the burden of paperwork/information activities on the premise that excessive paperwork activity exists when the burden exceeds the value.

The development of the value/burden approach has shed light on several points concerning federal information activities that warrant emphasis here. First, the fact that information is either collected or used does not guarantee that it has value. This theme is explained in Chapter 4. Information use is not an end unto itself but a means toward an end. Paperwork/information is of no value unless it leads, either directly or indirectly, to an improvement in citizen well-being, and if information is to contribute to citizen well-being, it is essential that the government (and other public and private entities) engage in a continuing effort to establish national objectives. The value of information can then be judged within the context of that activity in terms of its usefulness in

1. problem identification,
2. development of options,
3. choices among options,
4. program design,
5. program implementation,
6. program monitoring and evaluation, and
7. program redesign and replication.

Second, several points stand out pertaining to the burden of paperwork/information. The burden measure must be comprehensive and include respondent costs as well as the costs of information activities within the federal government. Both are important in that both are ultimately paid for by the citizens directly, and/or as taxpayers, and as consumers. In addition, attention should be given to the psychological burden associated with responding to information requests. In some circumstances, it is likely that the psychological costs will exceed the respondent man-hour costs.

In Chapter 6, a second approach dealing with root causes and managing paperwork/information activities is presented, the comparative administrative practices approach, and the information activities of agencies with similar functional responsibilities are compared and contrasted. Three case studies of various regulatory agencies are presented in Chapter 7.

The assumption underlying this second approach is that the practices followed in the agencies studied would be sufficiently different to form a basis for evaluating and determining which administrative practices were more efficient and which less and how much information paperwork activity resulted. The assumption was borne out by the studies.

One agency's legislative mandate stipulates precisely what the nature of the regulatory standards should be, whereas in contrast, three of the agencies studied were given, in effect, carte blanche to develop standards as they saw fit. Such administrative discretion tends to result in excessive paperwork.[2]

Four agencies employ efficient screening devices during initial review to determine the appropriate intensity level of review, whereas two other agencies review all cases with the same thoroughness.[3]

In terms of enforcement methods, two agencies place heavy reliance on punitive measures such as severe penalties and little reliance on monitoring, whereas in contrast, two other agencies rely largely on preventative measures, such as monitoring through reports and inspections, and do not generally levy large fines. The preventative approach to monitoring encompasses heavy paperwork activities.[4]

In Chapters 8 and 9, two management tools presently used by the federal government are examined with a view toward increasing their information value: (1) federal management information systems (MIS) and (2) evaluations made directly by government entities and indirectly through contracts to private firms.

Concurrent with a recognition by federal officials that the tremendous information burden both inside and outside the government is a problem, there is an uneasiness concerning the necessity to act on important national issues even though sufficient and valid information is lacking. That there can be such a lack of information has been recently illustrated in the energy and environmental policy areas. As a result of this feeling, expenditures for the automation of federal agency information systems is now well over $3 billion annually, and federal evaluation practices cost more than $1 billion annually.

An assessment of these two management tools reveals four pervasive problems that reduce the value of these activities in relation to the burden. These problems concern (1) complexity and/or prolixity, (2) timeliness (or the lack of it), (3) specificity and customization, and (4) validity. Too frequently the information produced by federal management information systems and evaluations is too complex and/or too voluminous for the decision maker or the bureaucrat to use easily and quickly. As a result, one or more of the following occurs: (a) the information is not used, (b) new information sources are sought, or (c) considerable time is spent distilling the information. All of these actions increase the information burden.

The second problem is timeliness. Often the information is not available when a critical decision must be made. This is particularly true in the new areas of concern, such as environmental protection, in which the data gaps are enormous. In critical situations, such as the natural-gas shortage during the winter of 1977, adequate statistics are not available when needed. When evaluations are made, their results usually are used as a final grading exercise rather than as an analytical tool for planning. Such practices tend to evaluate specific administrators rather than present prescriptive information that could be used by a policymaker or an administrator to eliminate or alleviate problems before or as they occur.

The third and largest problem is in the area of specificity and customization. Investigation of current MIS and evaluation activities indicates a weakness in initial program design. Those in the federal government who request information, the information users, do not focus sufficiently on specific needs and/or do not communicate those needs to the people who are asked to supply the information, the "producers." In turn, the producers rarely take the initiative to determine what information is needed in order to make specific policy decisions or solve specific problems. As a result, program design often elicits data that are irrelevant or far exceed what is necessary. More diligent efforts need to be made by the information user to describe and the producer to understand the goals of each program, how the information collected will be used, and the specific end products desired. In this way the value of paperwork activity can be maximized and the burden minimized.

The fourth problem centers around the validity of the information collected. The usefulness of information activities depends on reducing the uncertainty of substantive quality and assuring the validity of the information as precisely as possible. However, the professional competence of the people performing these activities and the techniques used to collect the information need attention. When contracting with private firms for evaluation work, agencies rarely check the reputation of the firms or their personnel for such things as quality of work, adherence to schedule, keeping within the budget, and so on. In order to award the contract to the best possible firm, it is necessary to have current knowledge about the reputation and the capabilities of key personnel of each firm being considered.

Deficiencies in the collection and processing of data by the federal government have direct and major effects upon the public. Poor information practices that lead to the wrong decisions have a substantial cost to the public far beyond the costs of providing the information.

In Chapter 10 we analyze a different type of management tool that is available for dealing with information burdens, i.e., compensation. The chapter examines the possibility of requiring the federal government to pay the public for information requested. Making such payments mandatory may provide an incentive that could help to curb inefficient practices.

The chapters represent a starting point for dealing with inefficient and problematic information management practices. In our conclusion, Chapter 11, we present an agenda that might be followed by those interested in developing the themes explored in this book.

2
Bureaucratic and
Political Dynamics

The bureaucracy is often referred to as the fourth branch of government, an epithet that has been applied to other entities as well, such as the press. Historically, bureaucracy has progressed from being an extension of the "arm of the ruler" to a position of independent power and authority. One of the ways in which this increased autonomy manifests itself is in the desire of the bureaucracy to differentiate itself from other groups or strata in society.

As a bureaucracy begins to identify its own independent goals (or, at least, goals not strictly identical with those of the ruler or executive) and works toward achieving them, it devotes some of its energies to the explicit goal of securing and maintaining its own autonomy. An agency develops what many scholars have called "the organizational interest." Stockfish describes this phenomenon for contemporary American bureaucracies:

> A part of developing this kind of feeling is that each agency evolves its own image and style, which in any given time are a product of its past history. It simultaneously espouses its role and mission in such a way as to fortify and enhance its institutional status. . . . Every man likes to see his organization grow in size and prestige. If its size grows, the probability of personal advancement is better; if it grows in prestige, the individual enjoys an enhanced feeling of personal self-esteem.[1]

Eisenstadt points out that this tendency can be documented for bureaucracies around the world.

In most of the countries studied the bureaucracies developed to some extent an ideology emphasizing its own autonomy, and its direct ethical, professional (and, sometimes even legal) responsibility for implementing the society's chief values and goals, in contrast to the vicissitudes of the political experiences or of the arbitrary policies of the rulers.[2]

A bureaucracy's preoccupation with maintaining and furthering "the organizational interest" is not necessarily synonymous with a concern for protecting and furthering "the public interest."

Basis for Bureaucratic Power

The preoccupation with organizational interest is especially important for our analysis of information management because it lies at the foundation of bureaucratic power. When the great sociologist Max Weber first wrote of bureaucracy, he thought it was a necessary and an appropriate response to the arbitrary discretionary authority exercised by monarchs and autocrats. Weber felt that modern bureaucracies *should* operate more efficiently than alternative systems of administration.

> The fully developed bureaucratic apparatus compares with other organizations exactly as does the machine with non-mechanical modes of production. Precision, speed, unambiguity, knowledge of the files, continuity, discretion, unity, strict subordination, reduction of friction and of material and personal costs—these are raised to the optimum point in the strictly bureaucratic administration. . . . As compared with all . . . forms of administration, a trained bureaucracy is superior on all of these points.[3]

The development of technical competence has produced a bureaucracy superior in knowledge, "including both technical knowledge and knowledge of the concrete fact within its own sphere of interests."[4] This knowledge can be equated with bureaucratic expertise.[5] "Expertise" should be understood to include two components: (1) the knowledge and technical skills individuals bring to bureaucracy and (2) the information (data) collected and processed in connection with bureaucratic duties. The possession of

both components of expertise can serve as the foundation for an independent position of power.

However, expertise alone does not explain the power of
bureaucracy. In addition, the bureaucrat has official information,
which is only available through administrative channels and which
provides him with the facts on which he can base his actions."[6] Control over information resources is an important aspect of acquiring
and maintaining bureaucratic power.

Main Themes/Arguments

In pointing to bureaucratic and political dynamics as one of the
key "root causes" of excessive paperwork activities in the federal
government, we are highlighting the fact that control over information resources is the essential way bureaucrats protect their perceived organizational interests. However, it is equally important to
underscore how an analysis of bureaucratic dynamics can help in
identifying information values and burdens.

Because of the nature of the policy process (i.e., the lack of clear
objectives and priorities) there are specific "pathologies" associated
with the acquisition, processing, and use of information within
bureaucracies. Only some of these pathologies are directly related to
the production of excessive paperwork. Others are associated with
inefficiencies in management practices, which means the government's ability to maintain a positive balance within the context of
the value/burden calculus is reduced. The pathologies related
directly to the burdens of excessive paperwork and those related
to inefficiency are both important if federal management practices
are to be improved. In theory, effective management practices
would lead to the most efficient processing of information; thus,
there is a potential for increasing the value of information within
government. In addition, efficiency implies a reduction in the
amount of redundancy and number of excessive paperwork requirements.

This chapter concentrates on those bureaucratic pathologies that
are directly related to excessive information burdens and those that
appear, on the surface, to decrease information burdens but actually
result in inefficient information management practices. The pathol-

ogies that are directly related to excessive information re-
quirements/production are

1. The nature of the policy process – by not being able to specify
   clear objectives, the government is responsible for an excessive amount of information.
2. Protecting bureaucratic interests through secrecy – this
   clearly has the potential for encouraging redundancy (i.e., excessive paperwork) in government.
3. Protecting bureaucratic interests through avoiding embarrassment and risk to the organization and the individual
   bureaucrat – this results in the production of an excessive
   amount of information by government and an excessive
   number of requirements for information from the public.

The pathologies that are related to inefficient governmental practices, the indirect burdens, are

1. Favoring internal expertise over outside evaluation –
   although this does not produce excessive paperwork by itself,
   it does relate to inefficiency in government by not ensuring
   that the best information is available for decision-making purposes.
2. The inability to assess the value of information in monetary
   terms or by any other absolute standard – as a result, intuition (expertise) is relied upon and one can expect inefficiency
   in management practices to follow; in addition, information
   that is counter-intuitive is often rejected.
3. The tendency toward the misuse and abuse of information
   resources – again, this is related to the question of efficiency.
4. Reliance upon a single source of information that is known to
   be loyal to the organization's interests as opposed to multiple
   sources that may aid in reaching the best solution.

Bureaucratic Pathologies – Direct Burdens

1. *Nature of the Policy Process*

As noted in Chapter 1, effective information management is

dependent upon the ability to specify clearly articulated goals, projections for future information needs, and projections identifying
future problem areas that are to be given high priority. The nature
of the program-oriented policy process in the United States does not
allow for this type of management. A recent presidential commission on federal statistics highlighted this problem.

> The basic difficulty lies in defining the goals of a program. In the
> words of an official responsible for planning and evaluation in a
> government agency, "when researchers say tell us what you want it
> appears that they are not aware that they have asked the hardest —
> perhaps the impossible — question of government." While it is hard to
> believe, the government is simply not good at defining what it wants
> to do in terms of needed . . . research. . . . Any proposal to improve
> on the present state of affairs should recognize that the government,
> in general, can only articulate the area in which it needs information,
> as exemplified in the request. Tell me something about mental
> health. But it does not seem to be able to get much below this, at
> least not on a broad front, to specify questions which might have in-
> teresting answers, and which might be answered. . . . The inability
> to specify the question to be answered, i.e., specify the goals, of a
> program, arises from the fact that the issue of what the government
> should be seeking to do is basically ideological, not factual.[7]

Thus, the nature of the policy process and the philosophy of the
decision makers contribute equally to the tendency to not be able to
specify and/or articulate policy goals. As the presidential commission on federal statistics suggested, programmatic goals (the ideo-
logical dimensions) need to be articulated; information needs (the
factual dimension) will then fall into place. Daniel P. Moynihan
agrees with the findings of that presidential commission. He reports
that the U.S. policy process is really a nonprocess, that the U.S.
system is not policy oriented.

> the structure of American government, and the pragmatic tradition
> of American politics, has too much defined public policy in forms of
> *programs,* and in consequence has inhibited the development of true
> *policy.* In simpler times a simple programmatic approach was an effi-
> cient way to go about the public business. The problem comes with
> complexity. More specifically, the problem comes when society

becomes ambitious and begins to seek to bring about significant changes in the operation of complex systems such as the society itself. What is wrong is . . . the limitations of the program approach to issues which demand the disciplined formulations and elaborations of public policy.[8]

Both the policy and the program approaches try to articulate the goals to be achieved and the consequences of the various options to achieve those goals. The program approach is directed toward a specific, short-term situation, with the purpose of maintaining or changing that situation in some desired fashion.[9] The distinctive quality of public policies based on this approach seems to be their emphasis on and belief in a programmatic problem-solving process that has a contemporary time frame. The decision maker seeks to reach substantive goals through programs that, in principle, can realize the goals quickly and efficiently. This process is distinctive from a public-planning or a policy approach in that it concentrates on problems (and problem solving) in the present as opposed to more future-oriented concerns.

The policy approach, which is also concerned with goals and consequences, does not focus on one specific situation or problem; instead, it tries to develop approaches or frameworks that may encompass a large range of alternatives. One of the major propositions of this approach is "that from the fact that everything relates to everything it follows that there are no social interests about which the national government does not have some policy or the other, simply by virtue of the indirect influences of programs nominally directed to other areas. These are the hidden policies of government."[10] The policy approach, therefore, consciously attempts to outline the complex interrelationships that exist in society and to develop broad principles that may serve to respond to long-term needs. One program cannot deal with a large enough portion of reality to constitute a policy that addresses most or all problems that might arise in a given problem area. Moynihan would also argue that a mere collection of programs does not make up a policy. Most studies would seem to point to the fact that this shortfall of programs is an intractable problem that is further complicated by the inefficient information management practices and procedures of bureaucracy.

2. Secrecy

The analysis up to this point leads to the conclusion that bureaucratic agencies are most concerned with protecting their organizational interests and autonomous positions of power. One of the ways in which this is successfully accomplished is by using secrecy to control the use of information resources.

The use of secrecy serves the power interests of the bureaucracy and may be the key to what Bendix calls "the bureaucracy problem."[11] Secrecy affects information produced within the bureaucracy for internal use as well as what information is released to the public or other bureaucratic agencies. A bureaucratic agency's position of power depends upon other individuals and agencies needing its expertise, and this suggests that a monopoly on the use of information is the key to a bureaucratic agency's security. Stockfish contends that "because of the critical role of 'secrecy' the subject of bureaucratic behavior necessarily has a very high information or 'intelligence' content. It would be astonishing, therefore, if the statistical information programs of bureaus were not greatly affected by bureaucratic motivations."[12] James Madison pointed out that the ideal state of affairs was one in which knowledge would guide decision makers in reaching policy decisions. "Knowledge will forever govern ignorance; and a people who mean to be their own governors must arm themselves with the power which knowledge gives."[13] Madison's statement implicitly assumes that in processing information bureaucrats should be most concerned with differentiating between relevant and irrelevant information as opposed to information that best serves their own interests.

In tracing the development of the doctrine of secrecy in the United States, Arthur Schlesinger points out that this country moved away from the Madisonian ideal as the bureaucratic structure became more modern.

> But events were conspiring against the ideal. As society grew more complex, government grew more powerful. The instinct of bureaucracy, as Max Weber pointed out, was "to increase the superiority of the professionally informed by keeping their knowledge and intentions secret." The concept of "official secret" was "the specific invention of bureaucracy" and officials defended nothing so emphatically

as their secrets. Involvement in foreign affairs strengthened the
addiction.[14]

By its nature diplomacy calls for a large measure of secrecy, and
military personnel must insist on secrecy concerning the most important military programs or inventions as the "purely technical" aspect
of those programs gains increased significance (e.g., development of
new weapons, new radar systems, and sophisticated weapons and
war technologies in general).[15] In addition, the development of "intelligence networks"—closely related to military and foreign affairs—calls for confidentiality and secrecy.

A doctrine or code of secrecy develops feelings of "we versus
they, insiders versus outsiders, allies versus enemies." For the
bureaucrat, those who work against the aims of bureaucracy are the
"enemies." Within the diplomatic sphere it is easy to integrate this
philosophy into the goals of policy, and foreign affairs are often in-
fluenced by the idea of competition. As an example, during the Cold
War the United States was "number one," and there was a feeling
that it had to do everything in its power to preserve that position.
Any piece of information that could in any way be considered "sensitive" was classified as "secret." This was consistent with the
policy goal of trying to ensure that the "enemy" did not gain competitive advantage. The Draper report on classified information
makes it clear that the policy environment and policy goals of the
time led to a widespread abuse of the power to classify information
as secret. Some bureaucrats used that power and the philosophy of
"we/they" to cover up unfavorable information.[16]

The appropriateness of applying the same philosophy to domestic
policy is questionable. The "we/they" philosophy should not have a
strong influence in the domestic sphere, and those policymakers
should be oriented toward solving problems instead of toward the
theory of competitive advantage, which is "legitimately" applied in
the area of foreign policy.

3. Avoiding Embarrassment and Risk

Bureaucratic interests are protected by more than secrecy and a
control of information resources. Bureaucrats also engage in activities that are commonly thought of as "protecting oneself and

one's turf," or activities to avoid any risk or embarrassment to their organizations and themselves.

These activities are best illustrated by some examples of "routine" bureaucratic practices. First, bureaucrats react swiftly and predict-ably to congressional challenges and "requests," and most of the responses are information intensive. For example, when Congress was investigating how Medicare funds were being spent, HEW reacted by doubling the number of audits that were authorized "in the field." The intent of the bureaucrats was to overwhelm Con-gress with information related to the inquiry. Second, one regular response to a "priority policy issue" is to create a blue-ribbon com-mission "to investigate the problem." These commissions usually produce multivolume studies that record their deliberations. The commissions give the appearance of acting on the "priority problem," but they do not usually result in short-term actions that lead to an improvement in citizen well-being. The effect of these information-intensive activities is to delay action on an important problem.

Third, another response to a priority issue that Congress is con-cerned with is to procure information about the area of concern. This often takes the form of multiple studies so that Congress can be "well informed." Again, the agency or department only appears to be taking action. Fourth, within agencies one can find numerous memos designed to define the responsibilities of individual civil ser-vants. A bureaucrat will often use such a memo to prove that a par-ticular area is "not my responsibility" in order to protect himself against any charges of not performing his assigned duties. Beneficial actions and policies are not given priority over paperwork designed to protect individual bureaucrats.

Bureaucratic Pathologies—Indirect Burdens

1. Favoring Internal Expertise over Outside Evaluation

The preoccupation with secrecy is consistent with a reliance of bureaucrats upon their own expertise, a rejection of counter-intuitive information, and a rejection of externally generated sources of information.[17]

On the whole bureaucrats and decision makers (political executives) are hired on the basis of their expertise and knowledge in a given field. (Obviously there are exceptions; for example, a new government reserves numerous political appointments to reward supporters.[18]) To a great extent their credibility, prestige, and legitimacy are related to how much their superiors rely upon their knowledge. As a result, many decision makers are reluctant to collect or contract for information from outside their agency or even from a different department within their own agency. Individual decision makers appear to feel more comfortable with traditional, familiar sources—whose value they can assess—than with an agency or individual they have had little or no experience with and therefore have no basis upon which to judge the reliability of the information provided. This conclusion is underlined by Irving Louis Horowitz in his study of the rise and fall of Project Camelot. "It is a contention that conventional political channels are sufficient to yield the information desired or deemed necessary on policy grounds. It further reflects a latent State Department preference for politics as an art rather than politics as an object of science."[19]

Halperin points to another dimension of the same phenomenon—the strong preference of career officials to defer to expertise. "Their own involvement and influence depend in large part on other officials deferring to their expertise. To challenge the expertise of another career group is to risk retaliation. Thus, Foreign Service officers have been extremely reluctant to challenge the military on strategic questions or to challenge Treasury officials on economic matters."[20] Officials defer to the expertise of others in the expectation that they will be likewise deferred to in what is considered to be their specialty. Without a doubt, this tendency has a major effect on what information is considered to be useful and meaningful by decision makers and other users in the federal government.

Deference to expert opinion is based on the belief that the process of reasoning by which experts reach their conclusions is impenetrable by outsiders.[21] To the extent that (1) the experts are members of the bureaucracy and (2) decision makers rely on "their expert opinion," the bureaucracy is successful in protecting its interests and position of power. Robert L. Lovett, who once served in the State Department and the Department of Defense, clearly states the bureaucratic point of view.

> Civilian and military executives alike should stick to the field in which they have special training and aptitudes; if they do, the chance of making the machinery work is excellent. One of the few humans as exasperating as a civilian businessman who suddenly becomes an expert on military strategy is the military adviser who magically becomes an expert in some highly sophisticated production problem in which he has no background or experience.[22]

It is also clear that the judgment of what constitutes "meaningful information" is more closely related to values and insulation of power than it is to science or the "objective, technical" quality of information. Thus, what is considered meaningful is closely tied to the individual decision maker and his values. With respect to this point, Richard Rose contends that "the more salient the information is to the core values of the policy-maker, the greater his use for it. The greater the incongruence between the value connotations of information and the values of a policymaker, the less is his use for it."[23] Sartori makes the same point.

> The stronger and more interconnected a policy-maker's values, i.e., the more ideological his outlook, then the less a man's mind is open to new sources of information. He does not need to be told more, because he knows deductively and as a matter of belief, all that he needs to know. The most structured intellectual outlook, i.e., the most ideological, is likely to be that of the expert, whose professional training will make him predisposed to recognize some types of information and not others.[24]

We would raise the questions, How well defined is the ideology? Is it commonly understood? and, most importantly, Whose ultimate objectives are being served when one behaves in a manner that is consistent with the ideology?

Clearly there is a relationship between the tendency to rely on expertise and to not collect other information and the nature of the policy process. Most federal decision making is constrained by time and cost considerations. Decisions must be reached quickly and should be subject to the least possible risk. Given these constraints, the influence of established policies and interests will be greater than any other resource open to decision makers.[25]

Because of these influences, federal decision makers have little desire to collect "new information." Robert A. Levine reports that bureaucrats and decision makers have consistently resisted developing knowledge (information) producing capabilities for many of the reasons already outlined.

> Time and time again, federal agencies at the top have tried to impose nationwide data systems; they have always failed. They have failed because of the very limited possibility of forcing the operating bureaucrats to provide data in which they were not interested and because of the complete impossibility of forcing them to make the data accurate. . . . The paradox that was never solved was that the simplest data system that could be designed was far more complicated than the most complex that could be executed in the field.[26]

In addition, a recent study by Caplan shows that bureaucrats will reject information that they consider to be counter-intuitive.

> Many respondents who rejected policy-relevant information did so because they found the results to contradict what they considered to be true. For example, they are impressed by the concepts of democratic leadership and organizational management, and the data supporting these ideas, but given the nature and pressures of their situations, many upper level officials were convinced that such approaches to management would be doomed to disaster. To illustrate further, although the evaluation of some governmental programs showed failure, program administrators and sponsors remained convinced that the programs had succeeded.[27]

2. Inability to Assess the Value of Information

In addition to relating our concern for the values and burdens of information in relation to the policymaking process, it is also important to consider the fact that information is viewed as a costly and scarce resource. The burdens on the public of information collection are often disregarded; indeed, costs are rarely taken into account in requesting information from the public. In terms of calculating costs, there are only limited organizational resources available that can be devoted to information gathering activities for any given policy or decision. The salary of any one official, or expert, is an integral part of the direct costs related to the process of decision making. In terms of scarce resources and high costs, there is a trade-off between the expertise already available and the possibility of acquiring information other than that they can be contributed by the "expert." This consideration is directly related to the strong tendency of bureaucrats and decision makers to rely solely on their own knowledge.

Because of the high costs associated with acquiring new information—including an official's time in learning to use the new resource—decision makers tend to not seek out new channels of information. "Once the investment has been made in information and an information channel acquired, it will be cheaper to keep using it than to invest in new channels, especially since the scarcity of individuals and input . . . implies that the use of new channels will diminish the product of old ones."[28] Once an organizational investment has been made, it is in the organization's interest to protect that investment or source—even if it turns out that it does not produce the best available information on a given subject. Thus, as Anthony Downs points out, decision makers are under pressure to reduce the number of data sources they use because of the time and other costs involved with gathering new information.[29]

As a result of a limited budget, cost/benefit considerations have become standard considerations in decision-making processes at the federal level. The use of cost-benefit analysis raises two questions with respect to acquiring information: How much information should be provided? and At what point does the cost exceed the utility of providing the information? It is very difficult to answer these questions when considering the use of information by decision makers because direct costs and direct benefits are not calculable.

But Ilchman and Uphoff point out that it is most important to consider information as a *political resource*. From a bureaucrat's point of view, information is a political resource to the extent that it is seen as a potential threat to the dominant interests and goals of his organization. From this standpoint, secrecy and confidentiality are particularly important.

> The importance of secrecy in politics and government becomes clear when we understand information as a resource. The value of a particular piece of information is crucially affected by whether or not

the possessor of that information has a monopoly. Once certain information is shared, its original owner experiences a sharp decrease in
control over its use. This is why secrets are usually shared only with
persons over whom the original owner can exercise effective sanctions. Fear of such sanctions reduces the likelihood of further
divulgence to others. The wider the distribution of information,
however, the more cheaply information can be acquired. A monopoly owner of a certain information can bargain to get a price approx-
imating the full worth of that information to the purchaser, but
when many people have the same information, each may be eager to
get what he can before another does the same. The price paid must,
however, exceed whatever losses might be suffered by the divulging
person as a result of sanctions exercised by the original possessor.[30]

In terms of organizational behavior, this type of value/burden
analysis teaches us that

1. The tendency to seek monopolies is a natural outgrowth of a
   concern over secrecy and a fear of potential utilization of
   forms of information (other than expertise) that others might
   possess.
2. The tendency of agencies toward secrecy and a monopoly of
   information leads to the foundation among agencies of operations that simulate a market mechanism. Bureaus within an
   agency, therefore, can be expected to complement each other
   in achieving their desired goals, trading information when it
   is necessary and beneficial to both sides as well as maintaining and fostering the philosophy of a limited use of outside information.
3. There are direct benefits to be derived from secrecy and confidentiality. An agency can benefit by exchanging information on a limited basis for other needed information; in this
   manner, it does not have to produce all of the "relevant information" from within. If the market mechanism is operating—on the basis of commonly held and understood assumptions—an organization can gain relevant information without
   feeling threatened. However, it can be argued that it would
   not be possible to initiate or maintain this operating procedure if there were not a conscious policy of limited access
   to information (i.e., confidentiality and secrecy).

Given these value/burden considerations and the consequences that flow from them, it is natural to not collect all the information that may be relevant to a given subject. The political economy literature is adamant on this topic. "In an uncertain world, rational decision-makers acquire only a limited amount of information before making choices."[31] Ilchman argues that the utilization of traditional political channels for decision making may yield greater benefits than the development of an information gathering capability as "Often the costs of collecting data are so high, both in actual resources and the cost of delay, that the ad hoc decision rules have certain merit."[32]

This conclusion leads naturally to the development of the philosophy that too much information produces inefficiency and bad decisions. Eulau argues "that a highly accurate, reliable and complete information system is not ipso facto conducive to rational decision making in a representative democracy. On the contrary, from the societal perspective, it may actually be so costly as not to be a rational instrument of governance at all."[33] However, from the standpoint of maximizing citizen well-being, we would prefer that judgments concerning relevance and efficiency not be made exclusively on the basis of maximizing the organizational interest.

3. Tendency Toward the Misuse and Abuse of Information Resources

Given the information management practices within the executive branch of the federal government, one naturally asks, How is the information under the control of the bureaucracy used? and For what purposes? The literature is full of cases concerning the abuse and misuse of information—information that could have been used to increase citizen well-being. Philip Hauser suggests that statistics are becoming increasingly important for decision-making purposes and, therefore, there will be a particular "temptation to use statistics for administration, agency or other interests, as distinguished from the public interest."[34]

Jerome Skolnick describes the administrative pressure put on police officers to increase clearance rates (the number of crimes solved over the number of crimes committed) to show "what a good job" the police department is doing. In response to this pressure, officers will falsify reports so they can show that there has been a reduction in the rate of crime in the categories their superiors are most concerned about. The phenomenon has been illustrated by the New York City Police Department.

> A Vassar College freshman . . . dashed into the West 100th police station last July 11 to gasp out an account of being robbed of her purse at knife point in Central Park.
> To her astonishment, she says, the officer who took her statement told her he was going to record the crime not as a felonious assault but as a larceny which is much less serious.
> The Officer . . . told her frankly that he was falsifying the report so that the 24th precinct—widely hailed as the city's model precinct— would show a reduction in the rate of violent crime in its area.[35]

Psychologist Donald T. Campbell cites two other examples of statistics being used for political ends.

> To return to an earlier example, Chicago's reform police superinten- dent, Orlando Wilson, was wise when he rendered the police records incomparable with previous periods. This may have been necessary as mutinous subordinates might have inflated the records just to embarrass him, easily done when a sizeable portion of crimes have been going unreported. Similarly, in these days many school systems are less vulnerable because their records and summary figures are "color-blind"; they in fact do not know which pupils and which teachers are Negro, nor in which schools Negroes are present. Records of overall achievement and trends over time can be selec- tively cited by politicians for their political ends.[36]

Alternatively, agencies under pressure may simply not collect in- formation that could prove to be harmful. Andrew Gordon and others have studied this phenomenon and report that "The Bureau of Labor Statistics abolished the urban poverty survey in the 1972 election year, and the federal administration, embarrassed at the numbers of people defined as poor, has been accused of trying to discontinue the poverty-level index. One wry critic has suggested that to protect themselves fully some agencies would have to con- duct business by word of mouth."[37] The same study also suggests that even if the information is collected, it may serve the interests of the organization to store it in an unretrievable form.

The data may even be collected in appropriate ways, but only be released after being made useless. For example, the sought information can be coded or presented in ways that render it harmless for investigative purposes. Data are frequently stored and/or presented in irreducible aggregates thus not allowing some questions to be asked of them; for example, police budget data could be available by police district, but unavailable by precinct or census tract or it could be reducible to only categories like "violence control" rather than to the specific amounts for "juvenile gang controls." Unless data are stored in their rawest form, which is quite unusual, some coding decisions must be made. The interests represented by those who determine the structure of the data files, and thus fundamentally affect what is retrievable (or retrievable at acceptable costs), are most likely to be the interests of the top agency personnel.[38]

Clearly, the incentive system—the system of rewards and punishments in bureaucracy—strongly affects the way in which information is ultimately used. Campbell contends that

The political stance should be: this is a serious problem. We propose to initiate policy A on an experimental basis. If after five years there has been no significant improvement, we will shift to policy B. By making explicit that a given situation is only one of several that the administrator . . . could in good conscience advocate, . . . the administrator can afford honest evaluation of outcomes. Negative results . . . do not jeopardize his job for his job is to keep after the problem until something is found that works.[39]

The present political stance in federal bureaucracies is just the opposite of what Campbell advocates.

In the area of foreign affairs Halperin outlines the dimensions of organizational interests and their relationship to information handling—potential abuse and misuse. He states that there are specific tactics often employed by bureaucracies to defend their perceived interests: (1) reporting only those facts that support the stand they are taking; (2) structuring the reporting of information so that senior officials will see what the organization wants them to see and not other information; (3) not reporting facts that indicate serious problems; (4) preparing careful and detailed studies that present the facts, in what appears to be an authoritative manner, in such a way as to bolster the organization's position; (5) requesting a study from people who will give the "desired" conclusion; (6) keeping officials away from others who might report facts that the organization wants suppressed; (7) exposing key officials, informally, to those who hold the "correct views"; (8) asking other governments to report facts that the organization considers to be valuable; (9) advising others on what to say; (10) going around formal channels; and (11) distorting the facts if necessary. These are all examples of ways information is manipulated and selected in order to best serve an organization's interest.[40] It is clear that in many cases, the organization's interest is not automatically synomous with the public's interest.

4. Reliance upon a Single Source of Information

The abuses described above are a by-product of actions by organizations that are primarily concerned with serving their own interests. If bureaucracies use information, they want to be able to resist any challenge to their organization's position. Thus, organizational interests may be protected by relying on a single source of information or a single methodology that is familiar.

In a lengthy article on the making of foreign policy, Alexander George contends that

> U.S. leaders have allowed themselves in several crises to remain dependent upon a single channel of information. . . . Among the many malfunctions of the policy making process evident in the Bay of Pigs fiasco in 1961 was the fact that Kennedy and his advisers, including the Joint Chiefs of Staff, depended on the CIA's estimates of Castro's military and political strength. Both were miscalculated and underestimated by the CIA.[41]

In commenting on the desire to rely on perceived expertise George concludes that "Washington's dependence on single channels of intelligence cannot be explained on the ground that the crisis developed too swiftly to initiate additional channels."[42] Clearly, additional channels could have been used, but they were not.

The result of relying on a single channel is that the bureaucrats report only those facts that support the position they want the decision maker to adopt or the position they perceive the organization has a stake in. "In this variant of the workings of bureaucratic politics the other actors in effect 'gang up' on the chief executive and try to sell him the policy they have worked out among themselves."[43] Clark Clifford gives an account of this kind of practice in the Truman administration. "The idea was that the six or eight of us would try to come to an understanding among ourselves on what directions we would like the President to take on any given issue. And, then . . . we would try to steer the President in that direction."[44]

Summary

As indicated at the beginning of this chapter, a clear understanding of policy directions and goals is central to efficient information management practices. Government has not received the kind of information it could use most effectively because it has not been successful in communicating its needs. A State Department study shows that in the case of Peru in the 1960s the government received only technical reports, general information, and abstract studies because of the fundamental misperceptions that existed with respect to what U.S. policy was. Thus, no one felt that they understood what was required.[45] (This is often true for domestic policy as well.) This state of affairs represents a breakdown in communication and reinforces the critical role assigned an organization's in-house sources of information.

Before becoming secretary of state, Henry Kissinger wrote that decision makers responsible for the formulation of foreign policy had a non-policy-oriented perspective. Leaders spend too much time getting elected and cannot think about policy alternatives; furthermore, the typical leader has no image of what he wants to do after he gets in office.[46] The lower-level bureaucrats are forced to rely on their intuition and experience; top-level decision makers often are not sure of what their priorities and interests are, and so lower-level bureaucrats are not sure what information they should be feeding to their superiors.

Moreover, many high-level decision makers are not convinced that the lower-level bureaucrats should become directly involved in decision making. There are a number of factors that are operational in determining this attitude. There is the desire to avoid the elaborate information distribution procedures; it is felt that not everyone in Washington should know that a decision is being made. Many government reporting systems require that many officials be given clearance and "sign off" before information can be released and/or sent up the decision-making hierarchy, and this elaborate procedure for transmitting information increases the likelihood that information will be selectively reported and/or "leaked." Given this likelihood and the traditional concern for secrecy and confidentiality, it is logical (from the political executive's point of view) to exclude the bureaucracy from the central decision making. Higher officials believe the bureaucracy is most effective in dealing with routine matters that do not require creativity and innovation.[47] Kissinger summed up all of these components quite well when he stated:

> Because management of the bureaucracy takes so much energy and precisely because changing course is so difficult, many of the most important decisions are taken by extra-bureaucratic means. Some of the key decisions are kept to a very small circle while the bureaucracy happily continues working away in ignorance of the fact that a decision is being made in a particular area. One reason for keeping the decisions to small groups is that when bureaucracies are so unwieldy and when their internal morale becomes a serious problem, an unpopular decision may be fought by brutal means, such as leaks to the press or to congressional committees. Thus, the only way secrecy can be kept is to exclude from the making of the decision all those who are theoretically charged with carrying it out. . . .
> The relevant part of the bureaucracy, because it is being excluded from the making of a particular decision, continues with great intensity sending out cables, thereby distorting the effort with the best intentions in the world. You cannot stop them from doing this because you do not tell them what is going on.[48]

This attitude on the part of political executives reinforces the bureaucratic pathologies, which produces a negative balance in the value/burden balance sheet.

3
Counter-Incentives and Other Information Control Techniques

Introduction

There are several things you might do about a broken television set including commanding it to work or destroying it in a rage. These options are probably suboptimal. Although the "command" and/or "destroy" approaches might offer temporary satisfaction to the ego, they will not cause the television set to work. The more sensible way to approach the problem involves taking the time to understand why the set does not work and developing a counter-strategy based on that understanding.

In this regard, government efforts to improve information management practices have been derelict. Time is rarely taken to understand the causes of bad information practices. Instead, commands are issued, and "policing" commissions are established. As a result, the policies adopted to deal with the problem have had short-lived positive consequences, and sometimes some unforeseen negative ones. To cite but one example of the latter, the White House recently "commanded" that the number of federal reports be reduced by 10 percent.[1] This was done, but the estimate of the number of man-hours needed to complete the reports increased!

One purpose of this chapter is to illustrate how incentives might be chosen and applied to improve federal information practices. The process should begin with a review of the primary causes of information/paperwork excesses, which would provide a basis for determining which incentives would be most effective in generating good information practices.

In Chapters 1 and 2, the federal government is characterized as a grouping of organizations and individuals competing for power and control with increasing citizen well-being only a secondary objective. In this competitive setting, information, which monetarily is relatively inexpensive for federal officials to acquire, is useful both as a bartering commodity and as a legitimizing, defensive weapon. When the increasing of citizen well-being is not given the highest priority and when the respondent burden is given hardly any attention, it is predictable that significant information/paperwork excesses will occur.

The first two chapters also documented the presence of other incentives that have led to bad information practices. Government officials are rewarded for loyalty to their agencies, which frequently is put above the national interest. "Whistle-blowing" and the leaking of information can result in the loss of one's job if the power and reputation of one's agency suffers as a result. Loyalty to one's own agency also leads to information distortions: evaluations are sometimes rigged and false information issued, all in the name of one's organization. When members of the executive branch testify on Capitol Hill, they rarely do so in the spirit of a frank and open exchange. Usually the main intention is to present an agency in the best possible light; Congress is seen as the enemy. Loyalty to one's agency is of utmost importance to a federal official, and the result is a sacrifice of citizen well-being.

Much has been written about the executive/congressional struggles and the bureaucratic battles within each branch. The infighting is fierce: in Congress, the fights focus on committee jurisdictions; in the executive, considerable time is spent on developing programs to move agencies into areas that traditionally have been the "turf" of other agencies. These contests generate tremendous information demands. The executive, in anticipation of challenges from Congress, generates large amounts of information to defend its positions. Congress, in turn, counters both by developing its own information sources and by demanding additional information from the executive branch. Within the executive, inter- and intra-agency power struggles at both the political and bureaucratic levels generate tremendous information demands both for "defense" and for new initiatives, and within the Congress, jurisdictional and substantive battles among various committees and subcommittees generate a demand for information.

It would be an exaggeration to say that ambitions for power, control, and defense are the only reasons for the imposition of excessive information demands on the public. Even without these pressures, effective information management calls for professional skills and a significant commitment of time on the part of the policymakers. However, if the incentive structure depicted above remains dominant, it would be foolhardy for federal policymakers to spend the requisite resources and time on trying to improve information management.

Current Efforts to Curb Information Excesses

Currently the primary method used to curb excessive information demands is the Office of Management and Budget's (OMB) clearance process required by the Federal Reports Act.[2] At best, this process is only a preventative measure; it delays and sometimes blocks government information requests that would put an unnecessary burden on the public. However, many agencies are exempt from the clearance review, and those that are subjected to it have found ways around it. For example, the federal government can either get research done under contract or by grant. A questionnaire to be used by a contractor must be cleared; a questionnaire to be used by a grantee is not subjected to the clearance review. Further, the review comes so late in the research process that the OMB is usually left with a "take-it-or-leave-it" situation. Even if the OMB could be involved at an earlier stage, manpower limitations make it impossible for that agency to spend much time in thinking constructively about ways the burden might be reduced.

Within most agencies, there are occasional flurries of activity, often in response to yet another White House directive, to reduce information excesses. But these soon fade as the desire of agencies to defend their actions before Congress and to expand their roles within the executive comes to the fore.

Summarizing the above, there are strong incentives within the federal bureaucracy that lead to the generation of excessive federal paperwork/information demands. Efforts to counter these tendencies to excess will result in only short-term palliatives unless the incentives to excess are confronted directly. With this in mind, we now turn to a consideration of other steps that might be or have been taken to curb paperwork/information excesses.

Possible Actions

Counter-Incentives

It is possible to categorize recommended changes under two major headings: counter-incentives and other information control techniques. Counter-incentives may be defined as actions to motivate politicians and bureaucrats to employ sensible information management techniques. In this sense such incentives would run counter to the current dominant power/control incentives for information excesses. In contrast, techniques may be defined as actions that well-motivated politicians and bureaucrats might take to curb information excesses. Counter-incentives might be

1. commands,
2. public hangings,
3. public awards,
4. ombudsmen,
5. impact statements and clearances,
6. task forces,
7. commissions,
8. compensation,
9. sunset provisions, or
10. actions to facilitate statutory revisions.

There is no question that White House commands, if well-drafted and taken seriously, could have a significant short-term impact on paperwork/information practices. However it is extremely difficult to conceive of what command could have the desired long-term effect. Federal bureaucracies have shown great ingenuity in their ability to work around commands for quantitative cutbacks in paperwork/information activities, and qualitative commands often generate a lot of activity with little final impact.

A serious drawback to the command approach is the heretofore correct bureaucratic assessment that paperwork/information cutbacks are not a high priority item at the White House, despite rhetoric to the contrary. Experience suggests that when the White House is challenged by either the Congress or the media, its own information demands become unbounded. Undoubtedly the federal bureaucrats would take the White House more seriously if it occasionally held a "public hanging" of government officials who work against the letter and spirit of the commands. But given its own very real ambivalence concerning information demands, it is unlikely that the White House will ever go to that extreme.

If public hangings are thought of as sticks, public awards for effective information management might be thought of as carrots. Award programs have been instituted for medium-level bureaucrats, but unfortunately, they are not operative at the level on which critical policy decisions are made. Awards for top-level personnel have not been instituted nor should one expect that they ever will be since top management gives only a low priority to the problem of information excesses.

It could be argued that agency ombudsmen are needed to represent the public on agency information request issues, but the record for such efforts is mixed. For example, there is an office within the Civil Aeronautics Board that has been able to maintain its independence and have some effect on the outcome of rate and routing decisions. In contrast, other agencies have established offices to review information requests, but they have ended up documenting all such requests. From the experiences to date, it appears that if an ombudsman office is to be effective, an open line to the public must be maintained.

If an ombudsman can end up serving the needs of the agency he is intended to watch over instead of the needs of the public, the problem is potentially even more serious in the case of clearance offices or agency-funded impact statements. With no direct input from the public, it is even more likely that such activities end up rationalizing all agency information requests. This, of course, is done in lengthy reports paid for by the public.

Interagency task forces have been used in the past in an effort to curb information excesses. Although such forums may be useful for the exchange of information, they have not been effective in reforming information practices. Indeed, task forces are usually appointed to provide the appearance of action and concern. Almost inevitably, the result is many meetings and no results. Task-force efforts will be marginal until there is real support from the top.

Through the years, presidential and congressional commissions have been established periodically to address the paperwork/information problem. To date, they have done little more than temporarily stem the tide. How many remember the Commission on Federal Paperwork or the Hoover Commission that preceded it? The effects of commissions will continue to be only temporary until they focus on the underlying causes of paperwork/information excesses. Even then, it will take imaginative thinking and support from the top government echelon to achieve any lasting results.

It is reasonable to ask whether steps might not be taken to force top-level officials to give greater attention to the effective management of their paperwork/information activities. A fundamental problem is that the situation is structured so that the government bears only a small part of the burden resulting from many of its information requests. Citizens and businesses are required to respond to government information requests, and although it is both necessary and legitimate to require citizens and businesses to supply a considerable amount of information to government, one can separate out a special grouping of information requests for which some compensation is warranted. In appropriate cases, the benefits to be derived from requiring compensation are twofold: first, the information supplier would be compensated for costs incurred in collecting the data, and, second, the government agency, by having to make compensation, would be reminded that there are costs associated with information collection efforts. (The possibility of using compensation as a way to improve information management practices, is developed at greater length in Chapter 10.)

In recent years, there has been much discussion and some legislation proposed concerning sunset provisions. In essence, these provisions entail an automatic termination of government entities within specified periods of time unless their continuation can be justified and authorized by new legislation. There is a considerable amount of information now being collected that has outlived its usefulness. This is understandable as information needs come and go. However, there is a need for some way to terminate information activities that are no longer needed. The application of sunset provisions to all new information activities might have a positive impact.

Some unnecessary information is required by statute. For example, the GAO has found that it had to let three surveys on gas reserves by three different agencies go forward because of different statutory reporting dates and statutory confidentiality provisions.

A decade-old executive order requires that all contractors who have federal contracts worth more than $50,000 file written affirmative-action plans. A contractor who performed work costing $30,000 ten years ago would not have reported. The same contractor, performing exactly the same work, would now have a contract for $60,000 and, thus, be required to file the written report. In effect, inflation has modified the intent of the executive order so that smaller businesses must now file reports.

As a way around this problem, the executive branch might be given the authority to propose small changes in the statutes, changes that would become law if not disapproved by either branch of Congress within sixty days. The proposed changes would be limited to those that could be justified on the grounds of eliminating unnecessary information/paperwork.

Techniques For Information Control

We strongly believe that if the proper incentives to control paperwork/information activities are instituted, the techniques to achieve this end will soon be developed. Some good work on techniques has already been done, and a portion of it is presented in the chapters that follow. The next two chapters present a conceptual framework for assessing the value and burden of information/paperwork. Particular attention is given to the definition of information value. In later chapters, a methodology for using comparative analysis to aid in cutting out information waste in federal agencies is presented. In the remainder of this chapter two other techniques, uniform reporting requirements and improved brokerage activities, are discussed.

One of the principal complaints about federal paperwork centers on the amount of duplication and overlap that exists. This perceived duplication, however, is not actual duplication—reporting the same information in the same form several times—but a reporting of the same information in different forms to different agencies. It is this type of duplication that is costly in terms of multiple record-keeping requirements and the preparation of multiple reports. The development of model, uniform reporting requirements for each area in which this type of duplication is known to exist would appear to be a fruitful approach to the overall reduction of paperwork.

In 1974, model uniform reporting requirements regarding corporate control and structure were developed by the Interagency Steering Committee on Uniform Corporate Reporting. As Sen. Lee Metcalf stated while testifying, "adoption of these uniform report-ing requirements will reduce duplication and burden on business and improve the government's data base." The point was further developed by Comptroller General Staats:

> We believe it is impractical for GAO to effectively deal with the issue of "maximizing usefulness" on an individual form basis. On an individual form it is difficult to counter a sponsoring agency's argu-ment that additional information for use by someone else should not be obtained in light of the need to minimize respondent burden and the sponsoring agency's cost.
> In the long run, efforts, such as the one you initiated involving cor-porate ownership reporting, are the preferred way to address the issue of maximizing usefulness.[3]

On the surface, the development of model information and report-ing requirements appears to be a very promising way to begin eliminating burden and duplication and a useful step toward effec-tive data sharing. In actuality, there have been real problems in get-ting very far with this approach. The problems stem largely from parochial viewpoints, differing information needs, and privacy re-quirements, and as long as the responsibility for achieving results is delegated to lower-level bureaucrats, little progress will be made. Each agency can argue that its reporting forms are now structured in the ideal manner for its particular needs, and in seven times out of ten, they are correct. For this method to succeed, some agency in-dependence has to be sacrificed for the public interest, and it is unlikely that lower-level bureaucrats have either the intention or the authority to make such sacrifices. At their level, "turf" con-siderations dominate. Other barriers to achieving progress in in-stituting the uniform reporting procedures arise from the fact that even though agencies' information needs, as currently defined, may call for information from similar categories, specific information needs often differ significantly.

Uniform reporting procedures currently offer only a limited poten-tial for information sharing because of legislation concerning privacy considerations. It is believed that the rights of citizens and organiza-tions to privacy and confidentiality are better protected when information is scattered among a number of data banks than when it is centralized in one. Of course, one could argue the opposite: having the information centralized gives the individual or organization a better chance to monitor the files than is the case under a decentralized arrangement.

To summarize, the uniform reporting method has a limited potential because of different information needs in different agencies. And as long as privacy and confidentiality considerations do not change, and as long as uniform reporting is not given a higher priority within agencies, even the limited potential that does exist will not be realized.

As Philip S. Hughes, assistant comptroller general of the General Accounting Office (GAO), pointed out in his testimony to the Joint Committee on Congressional Operations in 1974, the information problem in both the Congress and the executive branch is "to a considerable extent, an access problem, an awareness and access problem rather than in a basic sense, a data-flow problem."[4] This statement suggests that it might be profitable if information retrieval and dissemination activities for the federal government were expanded. However, it is important to know the nature of the underutilized information. The problems rarely concern quantitative data series per se; there is a ready market that searches out nearly all forms of "hard" data. The problem areas involve conceptual and methodological approaches to policy problems.

A number of depositories and assorted retrieval systems have been developed for the federal government, but with few exceptions, they are not worth the resources that went into their creation. In part, this is because they are not comprehensive since government agencies are unwilling to take the time to ensure that their studies are deposited. The failure can also be attributed to the policymakers' lack of familiarity with large data systems and knowledge of how to use them effectively. Finally, the information specialist responsible for the development of a data system rarely knows enough about the potential users' information needs to develop the most relevant retrieval channels.[5]

Conclusions

We began this chapter by pointing out that information/paperwork excesses will not end until the fundamental causes for these excesses are identified and addressed directly. In our view, the excesses stem primarily from competition within the federal government where information is seen as a means to power and control. It is questionable whether anything can be done to curb using information to achieve those goals, but certainly nothing will be done until the elimination of information excesses is given a higher priority than it now has. The "piecemeal" counter-incentives offered would at least focus attention on the dominant incentives, and the techniques mentioned could be applied to reduce excesses once the will to do so is developed.

The Use of Information
as an Indicator of Value

> The post-industrial society, it is clear, is a knowledge society in a double sense: first, the sources of innovation are increasingly derivative from research and development (and more directly, there is a new relation between science and technology because of the centrality of theoretical knowledge); second, the weight of the society—measured by a larger proportion of the Gross National Product and by a larger share of employment—is increasingly in the knowledge field.[1]

From the end of World War II and for the next two decades, research and development expenditures in the United States multiplied by fifteen times. Between 1964 and 1969 alone, the percentage of the gross national product devoted to research and development increased from 3.4 percent to 9 percent, a greater percentage than in any other country in the Western world.[2]

Along with this increase, a substantial body of literature has developed concerning research utilization questions: (1) how much scientific knowledge is used in policymaking? (2) at what points in the problem-solving process is the information used? (3) what effects are produced by using information? (4) what factors or conditions are associated with its use? (5) what are the barriers to utilization? (6) what strategies should be developed to facilitate the dissemination and use of information? and (7) what mechanisms can be developed to make the decision-making process "more rational," i.e., reflect the application of the best and most relevant knowledge available to policymakers? In other words, given the resources being devoted to knowledge production and application ($1.8 billion per year as of FY 1978), there is a desire in many government circles to document the utility and the value of the investment.

Within the last five years, several blue-ribbon commissions on state, national, and international levels have addressed such research utilization questions. In the United States, Congress, the Office of Management and Budget, the National Science Foundation, the National Institute of Mental Health, the National Institute of Education, the National Aeronautics and Space Administration, the National Academy of Sciences, the National Academy of Public Administration, and several private foundations have commissioned large-scale studies and made organizational and substantive recommendations concerning the issues. The Organization for Economic Cooperation and Development, Ford Foundation, Agency for International Development, and United Nations Educational, Scientific, and Cultural Organization have been particularly concerned with such issues from a comparative and international perspective.

Efforts to facilitate and promote the use of policy-related information are inextricably tied to the assumption that using such information in policymaking will result in a significant contribution to the improvement of societal functioning and human welfare. Efforts to promote such utilization as well as empirical studies of research utilization implicitly assume that the use of policy-related information (and research results in general) is of positive value. Few policymakers or researchers have tried to assess the negative effects of utilizing social science data. Similarly, questions of abuse, misuse, and premature utilization also have not been the subject of major investigations.

This chapter questions the assumption that use of information is equivalent to saying that information has value. First, information value is defined, and then the following questions are examined. Is actual use of information a proxy for value or, conversely, does information have value other than its use?[3] If use cannot be a total proxy for value, is it nevertheless some indicator of value? And, if so, to what extent? Assuming use is some indication of value, what utilization methods best measure this value and which methods are inappropriate? In light of the discussion of those questions, what does nonutilization show us in relation to value?

Definitions

In line with definitions used in other commission papers, we distinguish between data bits, information, and knowledge. The three concepts can be thought of as being hierarchically related: the term "data bits" refers to raw research results, statistics, and excerpts from articles and books; "information" refers to data bits that are organized in some framework (ranging from a very informal, loose organization to a formal organization); and "knowledge" refers to information whose intrinsic truth has been verified. Information used in this sense may include the following kinds of data bits: (a) recorded knowledge in the public domain such as the existing literature, the history of a given event, public records, and completed studies that have been committed to paper; (b) recorded knowledge that is considered to be confidential and, therefore, exists only in the files; (c) research contracted for by an agency including evaluation studies and surveys; (d) research completed in-house; and (e) research reports communicated orally.

One is initially tempted to distinguish between the purposes, goals, and styles associated with information collection and application. Some will argue that such fine distinctions are necessary in order to specify value within a context that will be meaningful, valid, and applicable to diverse audiences. There is no doubt that there are serious substantive and methodological problems associated with interpersonal utility comparisons, but the focus of this chapter is simply to determine (at a conceptual level) what general criteria might be useful in judging when information is "of value" to federal government officials responsible for the formulation and implementation of substantive public policies and programs.[4] Our aim is to provide policymakers and their staffs with a tool that may be of help in solving some of the information problems the federal government faces. Public policy must be made, and information will continue to play some role in influencing the policymaking process. Since it is not possible to come up with perfect tools, we are trying to provide some criteria that can be worked with and refined.

When formulating criteria for judging value, one is faced with the reality that the criteria must change over time. As a result, it may be difficult (if not impossible) to construct an absolute set of criteria that will be applicable in the long run. However, it may be possible to outline a process that can be followed in formulating criteria for judging value. In outlining a set of procedures that may be followed by officials responsible for policy formulation and implementation, we hope to focus the individual decision maker's attention on a basic set of criteria for setting priorities within the constraints of scarce resources. We are trying to provide government officials with a tool that will allow them to make priority judgments like the following: "Unless it is clear how information fits into a specific decision frame, it will be given low priority." In other words, we are trying to pro-vide guidelines for specifying how to judge information value.

What Is "Value"?

It is extremely difficult to establish an operational definition of value. Generally for the purposes of this work, information is of value if, and only if, its use leads to policies that increase citizen well-being and/or if its use contributes to societal improvement.

In terms of specifying what is meant by citizen well-being, it is im-portant to distinguish among the different motivations for acquiring, processing, and using information. One motivation, as the chapter on bureaucratic dynamics points out, is to increase the independent power and control of a bureaucratic agency; when this is the primary motivation, citizen well-being is not being taken into ac-count. This type of motivation is clearly not in the public interest.

A different motivation might be to increase the efficiency of ad-ministrative rules and procedures within the government. Such ac-tivities and the information needed to support them can be valuable in the sense of increasing citizen well-being if they lead either to im-proved government services or to a reduction in costs, and hence taxes, for the existing levels of service. There is no question that studies of administrative efficiency can be overdone or not acted on, but there is a possibility that they will be valuable if they are acted on. This potential is in direct contrast to only using information to increase power and control, which never increases citizen well-being.

In the case of government activities related to policy information and implementation, citizen well-being must be directly linked to programs and policies that meet some identifiable (and/or articulated) public need. Operationally, the value of information/paperwork for citizen well-being might be conceptualized in the following manner: information has value if it

1. contributes to the implementation, operation, and monitoring of federal programs that are responsive to citizen needs.
2. contributes to the regulatory responsibilities of the federal government.
3. helps citizens understand, evaluate, and implement what the government is doing and know whether it is acting appropriately and within its responsibilities.
4. helps citizens obtain government goods and services to which they are entitled.
5. makes an essential contribution to the operation of a federal government program that is responsive to the needs of citizens.

In order to construct operational criteria for judging information value that can be used by all decision makers and agencies, it is necessary to have a universal standard against which to measure value. In the case of public policymaking and the development of government programs, this universal standard must be the national goals and priorities. Information value can be expressed in terms of the extent to which the information helps to realize a national goal or priority; similarly, it can be judged in terms of the extent to which it helps to realize a programmatic or policy goal (if the programmatic or policy goal is consistent with a national priority). The extent to which measures of actual use succeed in allowing us to assess value (as defined above) will determine the utility of the concept of *use* for the purposes of this chapter and the work of the Commission on Federal Paperwork.

The Need for a National Priority Exercise

If it is true that information has value if, and only if, it contributes to citizen well-being, the operational process for measuring value must start from a continuing exercise that (1) identifies national goals, (2) establishes priorities among the goals, and (3) develops an implementation plan. As alluded to in Chapter 1, two deficiencies in the federal policy process that continually thwart efforts to measure the value of federal information activities are (1) a lack of co-ordinated goals, such as the tendency for the federal government to tackle problems piecemeal with results that are frequently disap-pointing or partly counter-productive, and (2) a lack of foresight, which causes the federal government to react to problems after they become acute instead of averting or mitigating them. In short, the federal government fails to plan in a systematic and coordinated fashion.

The criticism is neither new nor novel; what is new is the proposi-tion that the deficiencies are directly related to the problem of excessive federal paperwork activity. The failure to determine national goals and priorities forces each federal agency, each depart-ment, and each subdivision to determine its own operational ob-jectives and information needs. Frequently this determination is a self-serving activity and continuous information input is required to support the agency's existence. The price is excessive federal paper-work/information activity that has little value for citizen well-being. On the other hand, the development of a set of national objectives and priorities can make possible the necessary linkage between in-formation value and information activities and provide the starting point from which federal information activities at every level can be assessed.

Making value judgments is an inherent part of establishing a set of national objectives and priorities. Thus, those that are decided upon cannot come from the planning boards of the technocrats and the bureaucrats but must come from numerous public and private sec-tors. Consensus must be achieved through an "open" process consis-tent with our democratic principles, and all economic, political, and social sectors must be permitted to contribute to the determination.

After a consensus has been reached, an implementation plan should be drawn up that spells out how the priority goals are going to be attained. This plan should include a definition of agency/department responsibilities, budgetary allocations, and directives. The directives should be detailed enough so that all legitimate federal activities are identified. Information value can then be deter-mined as described earlier.

Once it has been shown that a particular program is consistent with the national objectives, the types of information that are relevant and necessary to that program can be considered. In doing so, the emphasis should be on distinguishing between information that is "nice to have" and that that is "needed" and between information that is "related to" and that that is "relevant." There are various ways to approach this task. One way is to consider the question at each program management stage. If program management stages are defined as problem definition, option development and selection, program design, program implementation, program monitoring and evaluation, and program redesign, government officials can consider information needs each time a program moves from one stage to another. If the same information can serve two purposes, redundant information centers should be eliminated. By the same token, if it would appear that critical information is missing, it should be added.

It should also be noted that the determination of national goals and priorities must be a continuous exercise, a process subject to continuous course corrections. As a result, information value—and information collection and processing activities—will be in constant flux and in need of constant evaluation and revision.

Unacceptable Definitions of Value

There is no reason to believe that the conceptualization of value that has been presented is the only appropriate definition that could be used. Indeed, within the context of policymaking and government, it does not seem possible to provide a universal definition of information value, so it is more appropriate to analyze whether information is "of value" instead of trying to formulate one general definition.

As indicated earlier, information is considered to be of value if it contributes to citizen well-being. In some recent work, the Department of Commerce makes an appropriate distinction between utility to the public and utility to the department. For the purposes of specifying and understanding information value, the distinction is particularly important because it helps to illustrate the necessary and sufficient conditions that must be met in order to be consistent with the definition of value given earlier. Utility to the department does not rule out utility to the public; at the same time, however, it does not automatically lead to it.[5]

The operational definition of information value offered above was formulated with necessary and sufficient conditions in mind. In the process, the following definitions of information value were cat-egorized as unacceptable because (1) they provide for necessary con-ditions but not sufficient ones or (2) they are inappropriate for the particular charter of the Commission on Federal Paperwork.

1. *Information that contributes to the effective operations of an agency.* One can argue that effective internal operations are necessary for the delivery of services that lead to citizen well-being. By itself, however, this is not a sufficient condition.

2. *Information that is collected in a cost/effective manner.* This concept of value focuses on the internal operations and ad-ministration of an agency. Cost/effective administration does have a potential link to citizen well-being, but by itself, it is very weak in terms of being a necessary and sufficient condi-tion.

3. *Information that helps policymakers set priorities and/or order agendas.* Again, this alternative definition points to impor-tant internal operations. In this case, one is dealing with a process that can order information in terms of relevance and benefit. Potentially, therefore, there is a link to citizen well-being, but it is not a direct link.

4. *Information that introduces a new idea or innovation into government.* Innovative behavior, like use, is not a substitute for value. It may or may not be linked to citizen well-being.

5. *Information that helps an administrator/policymaker justify a program or record of performance.* Here one is dealing primarily with bureaucratic justification and legitimization to superiors and to the Congress. If administrators are using information to justify programs in the public interest, then benefit is being provided to the citizens. If, on the other hand, information is being used to justify existing budgets and internal staff ar-rangements, then the focus is not on information that is of value. Thus, this definition is not useful for specifying value.

6. *Information that helps to assess public reaction to policy options being considered.* This alternative definition may or may not be useful in specifying value; it depends upon the intent of

and ultimate use by an individual policymaker.

7. *Information that provides part of a research base for future plan-ning.* The statements made about number 5 and number 6 ap-ply to this concept of value as well.

8. *Information that helps administrators/policymakers formulate marketing strategies for executive, congressional, and public presentations.* Information used primarily to formulate marketing strategies relates to legitimization and bureaucratic advancement. The direct link to the public interest is tenuous.

The above definitions of information value are inappropriate for public policymaking and federal regulatory activities because they do not ensure that information handling activities will directly help to fulfill citizen needs.

It is particularly important to sensitize government officials and citizens to the distinctions between acceptable and unacceptable definitions of information value. Unless these distinctions are clear from the outset, one becomes hopelessly entangled in attempting to differentiate between those information activities that are con-nected exclusively to bureaucratic objectives and those that are associated with the ultimate objectives (i.e., those that collect valuable information).

The way to make government officials sensitive to the distinctions is by setting national priorities. If specific national priorities exist, an official or civil servant can judge whether the information being re-quested (or going to be requested) is directly related to programs and/or policies established to carry out high priority national goals.

Since there are various motivations for collecting and using infor-mation and there are acceptable and unacceptable definitions of value, use should not be applied as a criterion for judging the value of information. Nonutilization of information should not be auto-matically equated with negative value as it may merely reflect a de-sire to protect "bureaucratic turf."[6]

Measures of Utilization and Their Effectiveness

Given this discussion, it is important to ask, What can measures of utilization teach us about judging whether information is of value? In general, the available studies on the use of information/paperwork by policymakers at the national level provide better indicators for the alternative definitions of value than they do for value as it relates to the public interest.

For our discussion of information value, utilization studies are quite troublesome because agencies as well as individual decision makers can always find a use for information – especially if a budget, staff, or other resource allocation might be affected by that use. In this sense, many utilization studies serve bureaucratic interests more than they help benefit the public interest. Thus, in terms of formulating criteria for judging information value, most utilization studies are unacceptable.[7]

Studies of the actual use of information tend to focus on a set of descriptive questions: Is a particular research study or type of analysis used? At what level in the decision-making hierarchy is it being used? How is the information being used? What impact, if any, does the information have? What are the barriers to utilization? and How can utilization be increased? These questions assume that use is good and positive; more importantly, they assume that use needs to be facilitated and increased. Even when impact is being considered, little assessment is made of the reasons for the use and the relationship of such use to overall policy goals and priorities.

Impact measures have been designed to go beyond statements that specify only the types of information that have been used; they try to specify how it has been used. For example, Caplan, Morrison, and Stambaugh measure impact by asking, Does the information used apply to a policy issue affecting the nation as a whole, an issue affecting a large portion of the population, an issue affecting one segment of the population, or an issue related to the internal management of a governmental agency?[8] Some people try to measure impact by considering what stage of the policymaking process the information is used in (i.e., problem definition, policy formulation, policy implementation, evaluation, etc.) or what role the information plays in the policymaking process.[9]

Havelock has tried to introduce a different way to measure impact by examining the amount of agreement between researchers and decision makers about the priorities that should be assigned to research.[10] Other descriptive, empirical measures of impact include extensive citation analyses, the number of different uses made of one study, and budgetary analyses of research and development (R&D) expenditures by agencies over time.[11] In the area of the adoption of innovations, impact is thought of in terms of the rapidity with which an innovation spreads.[12]

Each of the various ways to measure and analyze impact focuses on the relationship between researchers and users (clients) or on the actions of decision makers concerning utilization. Little attention has been given to the policy positions professed by the public or the responsibility of government to meet citizen needs.

Most of the studies make concrete recommendations on how to facilitate utilization, and that subject lies at the center of most thought that has been given to the meaning and significance of use. This contrasts sharply with establishing criteria for value. Given these reservations, it is important to discuss what the different ways to measure actual use can tell us about the extent to which information is of value.

Tracing the Flow of Information

Havelock, Calderone, Rich, and others have tried to trace the flow of information from the time it enters an organization to the final decision concerning its use (i.e., its end use). This type of approach can illustrate the steps followed in requesting, processing, screening, disseminating, and using information, and the key is to follow the process by which information travels through a decision-making hierarchy.

This approach to analyzing use is particularly attractive to individuals in and out of government who are charged with the responsibility of assessing utilization. The research methods employed to measure knowledge utilization can be characterized as reflecting traditional input/output techniques. According to the assumptions behind these traditional measures, one must be able to explain and account for outputs in terms of the original inputs to the decision-making system. Implicitly, this assumes a one-to-one matching of means and ends.[13]

The problems of locating and tracing knowledge as it flows through the decision-making channels and identifying its consequences are impressive. It is almost impossible to predict when and where a specific knowledge input is likely to have an effect on policymaking. Yet the traditional measures of utilization are based on the assumption that it is possible to predict when specific inputs will have an effect upon policy (outputs).

If one wants to go beyond the traditional input/output models, there are formidable problems of methodology and interpretation to overcome. First, because knowledge accumulates and builds within memories, some decisions (outputs) are made that seem to be independent of any identifiable, discrete inputs. This poses the problem of not being able to identify all the inputs that have accumulated over time in order to deal with long-standing issues. Thus, how is one able to judge levels of utilization and the processes affecting utilization? Second, because knowledge produces effects, it is often impossible to trace outputs back to their specific inputs, even when it is possible to identify the whole body of informational inputs. Thus, how is it possible to apply input/output analysis?[14]

Given its shortcomings, what can "trace analysis" contribute to measures of whether information is of value? Clearly the ways in which the utilization processes interface with the decision-making processes make it difficult to effectively apply this technique. However, it is equally clear that when trace analysis is effective, it can help answer some important questions related to judging value. It can help determine the extent to which

1. information contributes to the development of policy aimed at citizen well-being as opposed to the extent to which it contributes to realizing bureaucratic objectives. (Note: This helps clarify objectives more than it helps specify value. However, as already noted, the clarification of objectives is the first step in specifying value.)
2. accurate information is disseminated to the public as opposed to selective dissemination for the purpose of achieving other goals.
3. certain parts of the decision-making hierarchy are engaged in activities that facilitate value. Thus, it might be possible to pinpoint specific ameliorative recommendations.

In general, however, tracing teaches us more about the internal operations of government than it does about value.

Measures of Instrumental and Conceptual Use

When specific utilization processes have not been analyzed, utilization measures have often attempted to classify types of utilization. Caplan, Weiss, Rich, Knorr, and others have all pointed to one salient distinction; the difference between instrumental and conceptual use. Instrumental utilization refers specifically to cases in which one can document the specific way information was used in policymaking—i.e., specific data were used for concrete, identifiable decisions. Conceptual use refers to influencing a policymaker's thinking about an issue without putting the information to any specific, documentable use—i.e., it changes one's thinking about an issue, but it is not possible to point to discrete data that led to a decision. This type of classification is helpful in ordering types of utilization. In terms of value, however, this classification scheme would be helpful only if it were applied to citizen understanding and specific types of policies.

The instrumental/conceptual distinction underscores an important problem that one faces in attempting to specify value: the time dimension. Value changes over time so what is devalued at one point may be judged to be of value at another point in time. In this sense, being able to specify instrumental and conceptual uses of information may be of help in supplying an unobtrusive indicator of information value. However, one would not want to rely on this indicator of value because it does not provide an immediate tool that can be applied in the short run.

Information Use and Management Information Systems

The discussions of information flow and the problems associated with instrumental and conceptual use both point to some critical weaknesses in the assumptions made by those who advocate formal information management. The management information system experts like to think in terms of systematic and logical information flows. The process entails defining what information is needed, deciding upon a cost-effective manner for collecting it, collecting it, analyzing it, packaging it, and using it. The problem with this process as a model for a government information system occurs at the very beginning of the cycle. Individuals frequently have great difficulty in specifying the information they want, and a good information system must allow for this human weakness. The information experts' systematic-and-logical-flow model is unlikely to result in the collection of valuable information.

Budgetary Analysis

Another form of utilization analysis is represented by the assessment of research and development (R&D) expenditures within federal agencies. As Calderone, Wildavsky, and others have shown budgetary allocations are related to the priorities put on programs and policies by decision makers and program directors. Because of the effect of scarce resources, monitoring changes in R&D expenditures should at least provide a comprehensive picture of regular and changing priorities.

As is true for many of the other utilization measures, however, this type of budgetary analysis is not a good indicator of value. Priorities in budget allocations do not necessarily reveal anything about use and misuse and positive/negative value. Furthermore, as Wildavsky points out, major budgetary allocations seldom vary significantly from year to year. In addition, information value may be inversely related to levels of and changes in budgetary expenditures so that this indirect measure of use can be misleading. Levels of budgetary allocations may simply reflect an agreement that was reached between a bureaucrat and one of the congressional appropriations committees, and those committees do not allocate money on the basis of expected value.

Nonutilization of Information

It is probably safe to assume that 85 to 90 percent of all nonutilized information is not used because it is irrelevant to the goals being pursued by a government agency. One should not lose sight of the fact that potentially valuable information may be deliberately rejected because it is not consistent with organizational/bureaucratic objectives. It is also possible that potentially valuable information may be unconsciously lost in the maze of bureaucratic processing. Rich, for example, has been able to document two distinct "waves" of utilization of policy-related information and found that some information unused in the first wave was used in the second wave. These waves of utilization took place within six months of each other.[15]

Thus it is also important to examine instances of nonutilization carefully before deciding whether or not they are important to the task of specifying value.

Summary/Implications

The purposes of this chapter have been to specify what is meant by information value and to analyze the extent to which use is an adequate indicator for judging that value. As discussed, utilization research has not concentrated on questions that are directly relevant to the problem of defining the concept of information value. Actual use and measures of utilization are designed to answer questions that are of interest to those concerned with value in a decision-making environment; however, the answer to those questions provides only preliminary information in the search for what is meant by information value.

It appears that use is only marginally helpful in specifying criteria for judging value. However, we did find that measures of use are helpful in beginning the process necessary to specify value. First, use is a preliminary or rough indicator of value when goals are clearly defined and the information being used is directly related to those goals. (The restrictions place severe constraints on utilization studies as they are presently executed.) Second, by combining several measures of use (intended/actual use, trace analysis, instrumental/conceptual use), one can begin to obtain very rough indicators of value. Third, by studying intended and actual uses as well as instrumental and conceptual uses, one can gain a very clear picture of the levels of administrative efficiency. Administrative efficiency may or may not be directly related to whether information is considered to be of value.

It is clear that utilization studies can teach us quite a bit about the internal operations of government and the procedures followed in processing information. As a result, many agencies have relied upon such procedures as the basis for their thinking about "value." From the approach of realizing citizen well-being, however, that approach is unacceptable.

Since use cannot serve as an adequate indicator of value, we must concentrate on formulating a process that will lead to the specification of criteria for judging information value. In a fundamental sense, specifying information value requires societal consensus as goals and priorities must be agreed upon before standards can be established for the purpose of judging how much value information has.

Once goals at the national level are established, it is then possible to examine specific policy and program goals to see how they relate to the overall societal goals. What now must be sought is a process that can be followed to specify value for policy and program areas.

The Value/Burden Calculus:
A Technique for Improving
Information Management Practices

Introduction

Historically, information has been treated in the same manner as air, that is, as a free commodity. However, information is not free. It has various costs (burdens) associated with it and hence should not be collected unless some value can be associated with its use. More specifically, it should not be collected unless its value exceeds its burden. Although this would appear obvious, techniques to assess information value and burden have not heretofore been available and/or accurate. The common assumption is that information use is equivalent to information value. Such an assumption is erroneous and leads to inaccurate estimates of information value.

The purpose of this chapter is to describe a process that will lead to more accurate estimates of the burden of federal paperwork/information, and indirectly its value. After some preliminary definitions, the chapter outlines the economic burdens by following the flow of information from request formulation through collection, processing, and dissemination and then discusses the more illusive concept of the psychological burdens that are associated with federal paperwork activities. Finally, the chapter describes a process of thinking that can be used to assess the value of paperwork/information.

Some Preliminary Definitions

For purposes of this chapter, "burden" is defined as the negative consequences of the information process. This includes both the economic and the psychological respondent costs incurred in information collection and use. Paperwork "value" includes everything of benefit that stems from the collection, processing, and use of federal information requests.

It is important in considering value and burden to understand the meaning of "shifting," a term that has been developed in the public finance literature to describe the effects of taxation. For example, a corporation may be required to provide substantial information to the federal government. If we assume that the corporation can shift the paperwork costs onto consumers through higher prices, we would have to say that although the initial burden falls on the corporation it is shifted so that the ultimate burden falls on the consumer.

Information value also can be shifted. As an example, consider the value of the information that leads the Civil Aeronautics Board to allow a second airline to compete on a route previously reserved exclusively for another airline. Initially, the value accrues to the second airline, but in the long run it is reasonable to assume that airline passengers benefit from the greater competition through lower prices and/or better services.

The important point concerning shifting is that ultimately the value and burden of all federal information activities accrue to the citizens either directly or indirectly in their roles as consumers, taxpayers, or owners of businesses. Since the majority of the citizens are members of more than one category, there is a cumulative result, for both value and burden.

The burden falls directly on the citizens when they are asked to respond to federal information requests. Applications, certification, individual tax returns, and household surveys constitute the majority of such requests. When businesses are asked for information, their response costs are partially reflected in the higher prices charged and hence borne by individuals in their role as consumers. To the extent that businesses cannot shift their response costs forward in the form of higher prices, citizens who own businesses bear those costs in the form of decreased profits and/or net worth.

State and local governments also spend considerable time and effort responding to federal information requests, and citizens bear those costs in their role as state and local taxpayers. In addition, the federal government incurs major costs in planning and operating data collection programs and in processing, storing, using, and eventually disseminating and/or disposing of the information collected. Sometimes the government hires contractors to collect information; sometimes it provides funds to cover the expenses of administering federal grants-in-aid; and, in rare cases, it reimburses individuals and institutions for providing information. In all instances, the taxpayer ultimately bears the cost.

Information Burdens

Economic Burden

Various costs combine to make up the overall economic burden of federal paperwork. The major items include costs of initiation, response, processing, and storage. A typical information collection, processing, and use activity of the federal government, with attendant costs, is illustrated in the following:

Formulating the information request. This involves such activities as determining what data are to be collected, developing a specific collection tool or instrument, reviewing and getting clearance to use that tool or instrument, and costing out such activities.

Getting the request to respondents. This function includes data processing, printing, and mailing.

Costs that apply to both of the above include direct labor, travel and per diem, data processing, contracting, printing, mailing, and overhead.

Responding to requests. Respondents are required to bear (usually without compensation) the economic costs that result from their efforts to comply with information requests. The time involved may range from a few minutes in the case of a household interview to many thousands of professional and clerical man-hours in the case of a complex request for information from business or state and local governments. Other resources may also be expended in response —machine and equipment time, space, contracted services, etc.

Transmitting, processing, and storing information. Once received, information must be conveyed to the group responsible for processing it. Such processing may range from developing a simple set of tabulations to expensive and time-consuming coding activities, qualitative and quantitative analyses, putting the results into graph form, and the publication of the final product. In some cases, the information must be stored in letter files, in others, in machine-readable form. The costs associated with these activities, primarily manpower and equipment, must be included as part of the information burden.

Psychological Burden

Responding to an information request may also cause burdens that are not quantifiable in economic terms but are of sufficient import to be considered in an overall burden assessment. These can be called psychological burdens, and they include (1) all negative attitudinal reactions to federal paperwork/information activities and (2) all behavioral effects resulting from the negative attitudinal reactions.

Psychological reactions to any stimulus can range from very good (positive) to very bad (negative). As Table 5.1 indicates, reactions to information requests cover this same spectrum. For example, some people enjoy providing information, particularly when they are interviewed personally, and others want to have a voice, i.e., provide information, on policy matters. These positive reactions suggest two significant observations: (1) by focusing strictly on economic burdens, one might either underestimate or overestimate the overall burden, and (2) the method used to obtain information (i.e., personal interview or questionnaire) and the perception of what use might be made of the information can significantly affect the psychological response.

Far more numerous are the negative attitudinal reactions to federal paperwork, including the responses of individuals both personally and professionally. Hearings by the Commission on Federal Paperwork brought to light several negative attitudinal reactions.

Invasion of Privacy. An important value of the Anglo-American tradition is privacy. The U.S. political system is founded on the premise that the individual and society are independent entities and that there must be limits to the right of government or any other social institution or group to intrude into the personal affairs of individuals. As Esther Peterson, a Commission on Federal Paperwork commissioner, aptly inquired at the February 1977 hearings in

Table 5.1

Spectrum of Possible Psychological Reactions
to Information Requests

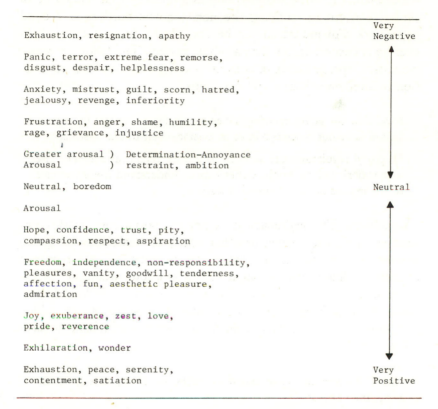

Exhaustion, resignation, apathy	Very Negative
Panic, terror, extreme fear, remorse, disgust, despair, helplessness	
Anxiety, mistrust, guilt, scorn, hatred, jealousy, revenge, inferiority	
Frustration, anger, shame, humility, rage, grievance, injustice	
Greater arousal) Determination–Annoyance Arousal) restraint, ambition	
Neutral, boredom	Neutral
Arousal	
Hope, confidence, trust, pity, compassion, respect, aspiration	
Freedom, independence, non-responsibility, pleasures, vanity, goodwill, tenderness, affection, fun, aesthetic pleasure, admiration	
Joy, exuberance, zest, love, pride, reverence	
Exhilaration, wonder	
Exhaustion, peace, serenity, contentment, satiation	Very Positive

Chicago, "Do you think . . . I haven't thought this through exactly, but in looking at the poor having to go through this, (complying with information requests), and in a way, literally undressed of all their ideas and the way they live . . . all this becomes public, do you think there is a trace of invasion of privacy?" The response to this question can be answered in the affirmative.

A recent law-review article on privacy notes some "chilling" effects of federal information acquisition: "The harms from unregulated government information handling can be divided into three categories: psychological problems created by acquisition of data, loss of individual benefits due to misuse of the data, and invasion of privacy *per se.*"[1]

Dehumanization. Dehumanization is a concept that should be of central concern in studying the noneconomic burdens of federal paperwork. An individual can be considered dehumanized when-ever he is treated as less than a whole person. The following state-ments are representative of citizens' reactions to supplying informa-tion to anonymous users and machines.

> I feel that the government agencies are trying to replace by regula-tion of laws our responsibilities as businessmen to our customers.

> Proposed regulations are written in a very technical manner. The vast majority of the public either cannot understand the intricacies or the impact of the proposed rules.[2]

Legitimacy. The legitimacy of a person, social role, institution, ideology, political system, or other entity is established by giving abstract, generalized moral approval to the entity. The importance of such moral approval is that it serves as a foundation for the ex-ercise of power or influence. The Commission on Federal Paper-work hearings heard numerous examples of situations in which U.S. citizens question the legitimate functions of the federal govern-ment.

> The FCC does not have statutory authority to regulate program-ming, but they do.
>   Instead of doing the job of administering a law that they (govern-ment agencies and department) have, they all get into the social reform business, and they don't just collect taxes, they get into the home situation business. They get into all sorts of things.[3]

> Time and time again I have had complaints from businessmen swamped with patently unnecessary paperwork requirements from Federal regulatory agencies. At times, these intrusions constitute a virtual infringement of their basic rights.[4]

> Government has, at the Federal level, crossed over the line from reasonable regulation to control and has become a growing burden to the private sector which includes American consumers as well as American business in a number of ways.[5]

In short, numerous corporations question the legitimacy and efficacy of government paperwork. Complaints center on financial and/or regulatory aspects of the forms; i.e., the forms cause an unreasonable financial burden and/or the information requested is outside the purview of government authority.

These negative attitudinal reactions to federal paperwork can result in a number of behavioral and emotional effects such as frustration, anxiety, fear, apprehension, and hostility. Testimony indicates that the complexity of some laws and the attendant paperwork requirements, coupled with the threat of legal sanctions in cases of noncompliance, often create frustration and fear of the bureaucracy. Federal tax forms are the most frequent cause of frustration and apprehension for many citizens, as noted in the following example: "I have attended conferences, conventions, seminars, and any number of discussion groups to avail myself of proper interpretation of rules and regulations; in most instances, I have been faced with utter frustration in not being able to obtain direct, definitive answers."[6]

Data forms required by regulatory agencies also create fear among respondents that they may be found in violation of the law. These emotions have surfaced many times in the Commission on Federal Paperwork hearings. For example, in the April 1976 hearings in Atlanta, the commissioner of agriculture for the State of Georgia, the Honorable William Irvan, noted:

> I am very familiar with the plight that the small businessman has in most cases when he has a limited staff to fill out this paperwork and to see that it gets filed on time, because a lot of paperwork that we have to file in the business community has a deadline. If it doesn't meet a certain deadline, you might run into some kind of a penalty from a Federal agency, so this is of great concern in this field.

Information Misuse Burdens

Unfortunately it cannot be guaranteed that once information is collected it will lead to beneficial results. Sometimes the wrong information is collected, sometimes it is improperly analyzed, and sometimes it is improperly used. In all cases, the citizens are ultimately burdened. Numerous authors have directed their attention to this problem.

> Over the past half a century, in ways not always known to its citizens, the United States has acquired the intelligence apparatus of a police state. Without ceasing to be a democracy we have allowed accumulation of the machinery of political surveillance behind the closed doors of unregulated intelligence, law enforcement and internal security agencies. These agencies, which exist at all levels of government, today monitor virtually all public and much private political dissent in the country. Aided by computers and teletypes, they store this information in quantities and disseminate it at speeds never before achieved. As a result, the possibility of authoritarian government has grown considerably while the possibility of revolution has all but disappeared.[7]

> Centralization of records by the computer and allowing dossiers to be built completely and permanently into an immediately available form makes ugly fascism operationally possible.[8]

Decision Delay Burdens

In some cases, the paperwork is so extensive that timely decisions are delayed for years. During these years of indecision, business investments may be delayed or denied, resulting in a hindrance or loss of valuable economic resources. In other instances, regulations concerning paperwork are inadequate. As Daniel B. Magrow, assistant commissioner, Department of Administration, Minnesota stated, "Federal regulations prescribing standards for program administration and for reporting often border on the disastrous. There are cases where regulations implementing programs are not issued until months after the first reports are due, and then frequently in tentative form."[9]

Concomitantly, the amount of information gathered by an agency or program manager may be so voluminous that it clogs the decision-making process. A mountain of available information may discourage agencies and individuals from searching existing data systems. Two negative consequences may result: (1) the decision may be made to act without benefit of available information, or (2) a new data collection effort may be initiated because the agency decides that it would be cheaper to ignore what exists and simply collect new information.

Cumulative Burdens

The total paperwork burden is important since even one series of justifiable requests for information can result in excessive economic and psychological burdens. This can occur when multiple federal agencies and levels of government each impose reporting requirements on the same respondent. In such cases, the individual burdens of federal forms from a particular agency need to be considered in the context of the greater cumulative burden and the ability of the respondent to meet the requests.

A good example of cumulative burden is apparent in a letter sent to the federal energy administrator in response to an information request.

> We are a small organization and handle small volumes of crude oil. The wells average around one-half a barrel per day. Any reports that we are required to file will have to be done by me which means that I have to spend less time in the field producing crude oil. I do not object to filing a simple monthly report, but there is a limit to how much paperwork we can do. Right now, we file a monthly report to the State Corporation Commission and the State Board of Health, a yearly report to the State Geological Survey, the State Agricultural Department and have at least a week's work filling out forms for the State Ad Valorum Tax Department. In addition to all this, we have the usual quarterly and yearly reports to make for Social Security, Unemployment, Tax, W-2's, K-2's, and the 1009 forms for the royalty owners.
>
> I haven't spent forty hours in the field since the first of the year—the rest of the time I have spent in the office working for the Federal, state and county governments. I work an average of ten hours a day, seven days a week, with a two-week vacation about every five years. It is approaching the point where I am seriously neglecting the oil business to do office work for the government. Our present daily production is about one-fourth of what it was in the late 1960s due to the price of oil and neglect.[10]

The cumulative psychological burden is most evident in today's widespread feeling of alienation, i.e., the belief that information compiled in ever-increasing amounts constitutes a control mechanism that ultimately stifles creativity and self-realization. Unlike the specific types of psychological burden that can be related to particular information requests, alienation is a pervasive burden that emerges out of the aggregate.

Feelings of alienation may lead to one of two detrimental behavioral reactions, apathy or violence. It is commonplace to identify public frustration toward governmental bureaucracy as an initial or underlying cause of political (including voter) apathy. Lacking effective political channels for the expression of frustration toward government, individuals turn inward. They no longer feel they have a stake in the system or a responsibility to it. Occasionally the feeling of alienation erupts into action, and citizens organize left-wing or right-wing movements that advocate and initiate violence.

Burden Estimation

Having indicated the primary burdens of federal paperwork, the question is, Are these burdens measurable? The tools and methodology for collecting economic burden data already exist. However, our investigations show that the woefully meager estimation efforts undertaken to date by the federal government (directly by the OMB and the GAO or indirectly through federally funded studies) can be wildly inaccurate, useless analytically, and far from comprehensive. Data on the comprehensiveness of OMB and GAO clearance coverage are presented in Table 5.2.

Most burden estimation work has focused on economic burdens, but even for those, serious inaccuracies are prevalent. The inaccuracies stem from a lack of precision: from a lack of a precise definition of "burden" and a lack of precise standards for collecting burden data. The following comment from a businessman illustrates how complex this question of precision can be in defining response burden.

> The basic point of my letter is that the paperwork burden is *not* just filling out of the forms (even copying it off the multiple pages supplied by the Bank Trust Department computer) but the correspondence, searching old records, telephone conversations, and

Table 5.2

Federal Government Clearance Coverage

Forms cleared	Percentage
a) OMB	3
b) GAO	24
Total cleared	27

Forms not cleared	Percentage
a) Internal Revenue Service	49
b) Other Federal Agencies	24
Total not cleared	73

Source: Peat, Marwick, Mitchell and Company, Small Business Reporting Burden, prepared for the Office of Management and Budget, 1975.

myriad of other activity required to produce "nonsense garbage." If a form takes 30 minutes to fill out, it is easily accompanied by 50 man-hours of related activity, as you can see (100/1 ratio of record-generating to form filling out.)[11]

To date, the data that have been collected are being used almost exclusively for accounting purposes; e.g., trends in burden totals are being examined to determine whether total respondent burden is increasing or declining. The data are not being analyzed in ways that would uncover such things as who is being unfairly burdened and what could be done to reduce the overall burden.

In the area of psychological burdens associated with federal paperwork/information activities, little conceptual and empirical work has been done. There is no easy way to measure the extent to

which federal information demands contribute to feelings of
dehumanization, apathy, isolation, and alienation. What has been
done, however, suggests that focusing on the economic burdens
alone can seriously distort the burden estimate.

Conclusions and Recommendations

The evidence we have compiled suggests that, first, serious inaccuracies exist in burden estimation work, and as a result, the value
of burden estimates has not been commensurate with the cost. Second, burden data collected have not been properly used; it has been
used primarily for accounting purposes rather than to shed light on
who is being unfairly burdened and on how to reduce burden. And
third, the conceptual and empirical tools needed to understand and
measure psychological burdens are just now being developed. What
little evidence we have suggests that respondents

1. are frequently scared and intimidated by complex forms.
2. can be frustrated easily if the language of the question is of a
   technical nature that they do not understand.
3. can be frustrated by overly structured, ambiguously worded
   questions to which they cannot respond in a manner that
   truly reflects their knowledge. They may sense that the
   answer options have been structured so that answers can be
   analyzed rapidly, but they are concerned that conclusions
   drawn from inadequate information might be misleading.
4. may consider filling out a form in order to satisfy the needs of
   some anonymous user to be a dehumanizing experience. This
   effect may be intensified if the respondent's interaction with
   the government is initiated or moderated by machines.
5. usually incur much less of a psychological burden if information is obtained through a personal interview rather than
   through a complex form sent through the mail.
6. often feel that the information they are reporting will not be
   used or will be misused to their detriment (this is especially
   true for businessmen).
7. may not be able to provide the data requested due to a lack of
   records or faded memory. This may produce frustration and

embarrassment, particularly if the information is requested in a face-to-face interview.

8. may become frustrated when asked to provide sensitive information about a third party, particularly a friend.

Specifically, burden data will not be useful until it is made accurate, until it includes psychological burdens, and until the clearance process is made comprehensive both in terms of requiring clearance on all forms and in terms of covering all agencies now reporting to the General Accounting Office. To further these aims, funding should be provided for projects that aim at identifying and measuring psychological burdens associated with information activities.

6
Comparative Agency Analysis: A Technique for Streamlining Information Activities

Introduction

Many federal agencies have responsibilities that appear to require coordination among agencies in working on problems that cut across traditional bureaucratic lines. It is, however, quite clear that department agencies use very dissimilar procedures to attain "similar" objectives. The assumption underlying the analysis described in this chapter and Chapter 7 is that at least part of the dissimilarity in procedure can be attributed to the fact that some agencies use more efficient information practices than others. The comparative approach described below is seen as a means to highlight more and less efficient governmental practices.

This is an exploratory study in a relatively new field, and it seeks to perform three tasks: (1) to describe and catalog some of the various ways in which similar tasks are performed in agencies, (2) to describe the overall activities that agencies are engaged in, and (3) to provide an analysis of the information/paperwork levels associated with such procedures. The comparative approach is seen as a useful technique for identifying administrative practices that are inefficient, for developing a set of more efficient procedures to perform various agency activities, and for demonstrating new research techniques for public administration.

For the purposes of this study, federal government activities were classified into four major groups: regulatory activities, service delivery activities, money collection and transfer activities, and information (research and publication) activities. Only the first two categories were selected for study because of limited time and resources. Within the area of regulatory activities, efforts were focused on three major comparative studies: health and safety activities—Environmental Protection Agency (EPA), Occupational Safety and Health Administration (OSHA), Consumer Product Safety Commission (CPSC); rate approval for common carriers —Interstate Commerce Commission (ICC), Civil Aeronautics Board (CAB), Federal Maritime Commission (FMC); and permission granting activities—Federal Communications Commission (FCC), Food and Drug Administration (FDA), Securities and Exchange Commission (SEC). In the area of service delivery activities, efforts were directed toward three agencies that are involved in conducting federal insurance programs—Social Security Administration (SSA), Veterans Administration (VA), Civil Service Commission (CSC) Retirement Program.

In some fundamental sense, activities of all agencies revolve around standards, rules, and regulations. Thus, the case studies focused on agency activities relating to standards and rules in the following areas: (1) standards and rules development, (2) standards and rules implementation, and (3) monitoring and enfo:cement. This progression forms the framework for comparisons and contrasts across agencies, and more specifically, the discussion consists of an examination of significant dimensions or considerations concerning each of the stages.

The following dimensions were examined concerning standards and rules development.

1. Specificity of legislation—whether or not the legislative intent and directives are stated clearly and precisely
2. Nature of standards and rules—do the standards address overall national considerations/objectives, performance levels, or process design features
3. Coverage of standards and rules—do the standards apply to all entities under agency jurisdiction or only to a selected portion of such entities
4. Rationale of standards and rules—are standards based on scientific data or on judgment

5. Public participation—the nature and amount of public involvement in the development of standards and rules

In the second stage, the implementation of standards and rules, five areas were investigated.

1. Clarity of standards and rules—the extent to which the standards convey their overall intent and their precise requirements
2. Intensity of review—the amount and nature of agency resources devoted to each specific case review
3. General petition procedures—the formal administrative process by which an agency is reviewed
4. Review staff background
5. Public involvement

The third agency activity stage, the monitoring and enforcement of rules and standards, encompasses the following dimensions.

1. Type and emphasis of various monitoring techniques
2. Relative emphasis placed on monitoring techniques (preventative measures) versus enforcement techniques (punitive measures)
3. Relative use of internal administrative procedures versus external federal court procedures in dealing with violations

The above considerations led to the formulation of the following propositions

1. Legislation stated in specific terms will result in less paperwork than legislation described in vague terms—paperwork required of external institutions and individuals as well as internal paperwork.
2. Standards that apply to process features or inputs (e.g., the design features of plants and equipment for the purpose of regulating pollution) result in more paperwork than standards directed at program performance or inputs (e.g., the amount of pollution allowed).

3. Standards based on scientific analyses (e.g., the EPA having to acquire data on the effectiveness of polluting agents) result in paperwork-intensive development processes.
4. Ensuring public participation in program activities is information intensive.
5. Standards stated in vague and uncertain terms lead to excessive paperwork.
6. Agency enforcement of standards and rules that emphasize punitive measures is less paperwork intensive than ones that emphasize preventative meaures. The fact that an agency is information intensive does not mean that it is bad or of little value.

In our analysis, significant differences were found among the various federal agencies.

1. The EPA legislation precisely stipulates regulatory standards whereas, in contrast, the ICC, the CAB, and the FMC legislation is vague, which allows those agencies to develop standards internally.
2. The FCC, the FMC, and the SEC have output standards that apply directly to product and activity performance whereas OSHA has input standards that apply primarily to process design features.
3. The authorizing legislation of the SEC calls for selective coverage only whereas, in contrast, the legislation of OSHA, the EPA, and the FCC requires that regulatory standards and rules apply to all firms in the regulated industry.
4. Decisions concerning regulatory activities in the EPA and the FDA are primarily based upon scientific criteria, while such activities in the FCC and the SEC are based largely upon the discretion of government officials.
5. The CPSC went beyond the public involvement requirements of the Administrative Procedures Act by asking that the public write the initial standards to be reviewed by agency staff while, in contrast, the initial standards of OSHA were exempt from such requirements altogether.
6. The ICC, the FMC, the CAB, and the SEC employ efficient screening devices during initial review in order to determine

the appropriate intensity level of review, whereas the FDA and the FCC review all cases with the same thoroughness.

7. The SEC places almost complete reliance on informal discretionary procedures, while the ICC, the CAB, the FMC, and the FCC rely on formal procedures that are more open to public scrutiny.

8. The substantive rate reviewers of the CAB and the FCC, who are primarily economists and accountants, base their decisions on precise economic criteria while, in contrast, the ICC substantive rate reviewers, who are primarily attorneys, make decisions based largely on precedent and judgment.

9. In terms of enforcement, the FMC and the ICC rely primarily on punitive measures such as severe penalties whereas, in contrast, OSHA and the FDA rely largely on preventative measures such as monitoring through reports and inspections.

In Chapter 7 these contrasts are explored in detail as are their implications for information management and efficiency.

Research Design and Methodology

Having selected the agency groupings for study, the following methods were used to collect the information necessary to perform the comparative analyses.

- Read agency literature
- Read privately produced information on agencies
- Consulted academicians and other experts in the field of public administration
- Conducted preliminary interviews with agencies to obtain a general agency overview
- Examined paper-intensity indicators in regard to GAO/OMB estimates of man-hour burdens; internal agency estimates of resources devoted to information collection, processing, and use; ratio of respondent burden to total program or agency outlays; and ratio of respondent burden to number of units regulated

The second step was to narrow the scope of the comparison to one

or two specific agency activities that although similar in purpose, appeared to be administered differently.

Third was to find out which people in each agency supervised and
implemented specific activities. Initially we read each agency's
annual report to Congress and utilized each agency's telephone directory. Then, to supplement that information, interviews were
conducted with a senior program director to obtain a general perspective on each agency.

Fourth was to develop a general interview technique and a standardized comparison procedure. Literature on the agencies and the
data gathered from the initial agency interviews were analyzed.
Four basic categories of agency activities emerged out of this
analysis: standards development, implementation, monitoring, and
enforcement. Based on this structure, an interview questionnaire
was developed. The fifth step encompassed the completion of all
agency interviews, a revision of the interview questionnaire and the
comparative study process based on the feedback, and final interviews based on the revised questionnaire.

The final step was to put the data into a framework so that meaningful comparisons could be made and conclusions drawn as to the
cost effectiveness of specific administrative practices. Similar agency
activities were isolated, and comparisons were made of the range
and effectiveness of the administrative practices required to carry
out each particular activity. Initial hypotheses were revised in light
of empirical data and tentative conclusions were drawn.

Conclusions of the Study

For the most part, the conclusions concerning various administrative practices and their associated paperwork activities are
obvious, perhaps even banal. Herein lies the strength of comparative analysis. In terms of administrative practices, "obvious"
means that this type of study has functional application at virtually
all bureaucratic levels. Once a comparative framework has been con-
structed, the data collected, and the comparisons made, the conclusions vis-à-vis paperwork implications are usually plainly evident.
Such comparative assessments can provide government officials and
other interested parties with a broad perspective on which approaches might be taken to realize agency objectives. Clearly this

can be useful in reducing paperwork/information activities since such a perspective can identify and eliminate unnecessary and excessive regulatory practices. Combined with the value/burden approach, which assesses paperwork activities more rigorously, comparative analysis can provide a basis for a significant streamlining of public administrative practices.

The conclusions presented below were based on four comparative studies.

1. Environmental Protection Agency, Occupational Safety and Health Administration, and Consumer Product Safety Commission
2. Federal Communications Commission, Food and Drug Administration, and Securities and Exchange Commission
3. Interstate Commerce Commission, Civil Aeronautics Board, and Federal Maritime Commission
4. Social Security Administration, Veterans Administration, and Civil Service Commission

To provide the interested reader with a more detailed analysis of the comparative framework, three of the studies are discussed further in Chapter 7.

Standards and Rules Development

The conclusions about the development of standards and rules in federal agencies were based on an examination of specificity of legislation, nature of standards and rules, coverage of standards and rules, rationale of standards and rules, and public involvement. Table 6.1 compares these aspects of standards and rules development by agency.

Specificity of Legislation

Legislative clarity is of great importance in ensuring that a regulatory agency follows a clear and legitimate course of action. While specificity can restrict an agency, its existence should also minimize information activity and paperwork requirements. When agency objectives are ambiguous, paperwork/information requirements are likely to be greater. An example of legislative clarity is the

Table 6.1

Standards and Rules Development

Agency	Specificity of Legislation	Nature of Stan/Rules	Coverage of Stan/Rules	Rationale of Stan/Rules	Public Involvement
ICC	extremely vague and broad legislation	technical input	full	discretionary	-
CAB	"	"	"	economic data	-
FMC	"	"	"	discretionary	-
OSHA	-	input	"	-	Initial standard exempt from Administrative Procedures Act.
EPA	specific legislation	national objectives plus input/output	-	scientific	-
CPSC	-	input/output	-	-	goes beyond APA, public asked to write initial standards
FCC	extremely vague and broad legislation	"	full	judgmental (discretionary)	input from broadcast lobby
SEC	"	output	legislative exemptions	"	input from Securities Exchange & firms
FDA	vague and broad legislation, except for Delaney Amendment	output primarily	full	scientific data	close assoc. w/the 20 firms which submit 65% food-color additive apps.
VA	-	input	-	fairly precise medical terminology. But open to discussion	-
SSA	precise	"	-	precise medical terminology	-
CSC	vague	output	-	judgmental (extreme discretion)	-

act establishing the Environmental Protection Agency. The act calls for the development and use of three types of standards: "national objectives standards," "effluent guidelines," and "process standards." In other words, the legislation calls for the development and use of national pollution reduction goals, effluent guidelines for all sources of pollution, and specific requirements for the types of equipment that can be used in plants and factories.

At the other extreme is the vague legislation specifying the criteria upon which transport rates are to be set by the Civil Aeronautics Board, the Federal Maritime Commission, and the Interstate Commerce Commission. The FMC legislation simply states that rates should be neither so high nor so low as to be detrimental to U.S. commerce. The CAB and the ICC legislation state generally that rates are not to be unjust or unreasonable, unjustly discriminatory, or unduly prejudicial or preferential. Similarly ambiguous is the legislation specifying the criteria to be followed by the Federal Communications Commission and the Securities and Exchange Commission in approving private sector activities. The FCC has been given power to regulate broadcasting in "the public interest, convenience, and necessity." The SEC must use the criteria of adequate and accurate disclosure in approving securities registration statements.

The lack of specificity in legislation results in broad speculation about and lengthy interpretations of permissible agency activities, which leads to excessive paperwork/information activity. The general legislative statements for the CAB, the FMC, and the ICC have resulted in long interpretive histories and legislative appeals. At the FCC, vague statutory language has hampered the development of a coherent public policy and has left the agency open to undue political pressures from Congress, licensees, and the general public. All these agencies were granted broad powers with few meaningful guidelines.

Nature of Standards and Rules

We have found that agencies use three types of standards in trying to fulfill their responsibilities: national objectives, performance (output) standards, and specific process design (input) standards.

The agencies studied employ various combinations of these standards. The EPA, for example, has all three types of standards: it has national air- and water-quality standards, it has emission standards for all firms, and it has specific design standards. The Consumer Product Safety Commission and the Food and Drug Administration have no quantifiable national objectives to reduce health hazards; they have only specific product performance (output) and process design (input) standards. The Occupational Safety and Health Administration has primarily process design (input) standards such as equipment specifications.

Process design standards are used to regulate medical eligibility in the Bureau of Disability within the Social Security Administration and the Veterans Administration. In the Civil Service Commission Retirement Program output standards are used. The former specify criteria for disability; the latter define disability as the inability to perform (as determined by a physician) rather than as the existence of specific medical impairments.

Although it is desirable to relate agency activities to specific national objectives, such as reducing health hazards by a given amount, in most cases this is not possible because there is no systematic procedure for determining national objectives and allocating resources accordingly. Even if this were possible, most agencies would still find it necessary to impose standards to control either specific product design or product performance. In terms of the amount of paperwork/information generated, it is less expensive to impose output restrictions or requirements (thus allowing those being regulated to comply with such standards in whatever manner best suits them) than to develop and implement input design standards. This is true because there are generally far more inputs to be considered than outputs. Recent work by the FCC Re-regulation Task Force supports this premise. The agency is slowly revising its rules to become more output oriented than input oriented. Increasingly the broadcast industry is told what it must perform rather than how to perform.

Coverage of Standards and Rules

The extent of regulatory coverage can have a significant impact on paperwork/information costs. If it is possible to protect the public interest by applying regulatory coverage to only a fraction of all those entities or persons who theoretically might be covered, it is less costly in terms of paperwork/information generation than if all must be covered.

There are significant differences among the agencies surveyed regarding the extent of regulation coverage. Regulatory coverage at OSHA applies to all places of work having one or more employees. The EPA standards apply to all present or potential polluters. Similarly the FDA reviews all drugs prior to their being put on the market, and the FCC reviews all license applications and renewal requests. In contrast, the SEC coverage is selective.

Although comprehensive coverage is more expensive from a

paperwork/information standpoint than selective coverage, the former is necessary if serious injury or death might result without it. This is clearly the case with respect to OSHA and the FDA.

Rationale of Standards and Rules

In certain instances, scientific data are of considerable aid in the development of standards. In cases where decisions are necessarily judgmental, there is less justification for such analyses. The agencies studied base their standards on both scientific analysis and judgmental factors. Those agencies that employ the more rigorous analysis include the EPA and the FDA; those that base their decisions on primarily judgmental factors include the FCC and the SEC. Other agencies such as the CAB, the ICC, and the FMC use economic analyses to establish general criteria for regulation levels and use judgmental factors in the application of those general rules.

Clearly, standards based on scientific analyses are initially more expensive than judgmental decision making. Also they are verifiable and permit a uniformity of application, while standards based on judgment are unpredictable and subject to bureaucratic whim. On the other hand, scientific data and analyses are inflexible, and the decisions based on them may be uniform but not equitable. More obscurely, scientific data may be used to disguise the use of judgmental standards. In terms of streamlining paperwork/information processes, care should be taken to determine when scientific analyses are better to fulfill agency responsibilities and when less rigorous standards are appropriate.

Public Involvement: Participation

Government decisions are bound to be better if all legitimate parties have a chance to be heard in the decision-making process. However, more participation is expensive in terms of the amount of paperwork/information generated. A considerable degree of variation was observed among agencies regarding public involvement in the setting of standards. In the case of OSHA, the agency is exempt from the Administrative Procedures Act, which requires public review of and comments on agency standards. In contrast, the CPSC has instituted an "offerer process" in which the public (both consumer groups and industry) is asked to write the standards; these are then reviewed and issued by the CPSC staff.

Although virtually all agencies are required to provide for public involvement in the rule-making process, the results are uncertain. Citizen participation increases information costs significantly, but the study indicates that such involvement can lead to an overall increase in citizen well-being. Much work remains to be done on how to make use of citizen involvement in the most cost-effective manner.

Standards and Rules Implementation

The conclusions reached about the implementation of standards and rules were based on an examination of clarity, intensity of review, the petition process, review staff background, and public involvement. Table 6.2 compares these various aspects of the implementation of standards for the agencies studied.

Clarity of Standards and Rules

To minimize paperwork/information activities, a minimum of discretion in decision making is desirable. Discretion means ambiguity, and ambiguity means that unnecessary requests will be made in the hope of getting approval. When the meaning of standards are well understood, requests are made only when there is a high probability of approval. Furthermore, only relevant information is submitted, reducing the information burden for the applicant.

There is considerable variation in the clarity of agency standards. In the case of the CAB, very little ambiguity exists between the agency and the airlines regarding the rate-of-return criterion as it relates to rate approvals. By contrast, in the ICC and the FMC rate making is discretionary, based on precedent and negotiations. In fact, both agencies argue that each case is unique and has to be decided on its own merits. Similarly the approval processes of the FCC, the SEC, and the FDA are discretionary. After more than forty years of existence, the FCC and the SEC are unable to translate their general legislative mandates into clear, operational standards. And even though the FDA describes its activities in a scientific shibboleth, the approval of food or color additives is really a matter of judgment. The differences in the specificity of medical rules also reflect substantial discretionary powers. The CSC rules are the most imprecise, reflecting only general criteria about what

Table 6.2

Standards and Rules Implementation

Agency	Clarity of Stan/Rules	Intensity of Review	Petition Process	Review Staff Background	Public Input
ICC	Vague	Selective	80% initially cleared w/out further processing	Attorneys	Agency representation of consumer viewpoint
CAB	Specific (based on economic data)	"	95% initially cleared	Economists	"
FMC	Vague	"	90% initially cleared	Economists, Accountants	New consumer unit w/unclear mandate
OSHA	-	-	-	-	-
EPA	-	-	-	-	-
CPSC	-	-	-	-	-
FCC	Broad discretion	Comprehensive	75% cleared w/out hearing	Lawyers, Engineers, Accountants	-
SEC	"	Selective	99% w/out formal protest	Lawyers, Financial Analysts	-
FDA	Scientific language masks broad discretion	Comprehensive	99% never requires hearing	Scientists, Lawyers	-
VA	Generally clear	-	-	-	-
SSA	Very precise, but not uniform throughout Agency	-	-	-	-
CSC	Extremely vague	-	-	-	-

conditions must be met. The VA rating schedule of impairments is less precise than the SSA schedule so that the decision maker can exercise more discretion than in the SSA, but less discretion than is permitted by the CSC standards.

A case-by-case approach to decision making that is largely based on precedent and negotiation results in a certain amount of rigor and clarity since consistent patterns usually arise, patterns that ICC carriers, for example, understand well and follow. Eventually, however, decisions made by using this informal process result in ambiguity and/or require the exercise of discretion on the part of the decision maker. Both elements are likely to result in increased paperwork activity. Imprecise ICC rules encourage carriers to attempt to push through many rate proposals that they would not propose if the rules were clearer. Imprecise rules also encourage corporations to submit applications just to "get in line" for review and to rely upon an agency's staff to request the necessary disclosure information. Because of the amount of paperwork/information that results from the exercise of discretion and decision making on a case-by-case basis, new efforts to develop more precise decision rules and criteria seem warranted.

Intensity of Review

Once it has been decided what and who needs to be regulated and by what criteria, consideration must be given to the intensity of the review effort. There are two basic approaches to the review of cases by agencies, comprehensive and selective oversight. Which approach is taken in reviewing cases has a significant impact on paperwork/information costs. As in the case of legislative coverage, if it were possible to fulfill regulatory responsibilities by reviewing only a portion of all cases—selective oversight—it would be far less costly than reviewing all cases.

In agencies such as the ICC, the FMC, and the CAB that have large caseload burdens, the review time accorded each case is minimal. Indeed, if one assumes forty hours a week, fifty weeks per year, and 100 percent of staff time devoted exclusively to rate approval activities (which is not the case), the average amount of time that can be spent on each case in the ICC is twelve minutes; in the CAB, roughly twenty-five minutes. Because of their excessive caseload burdens, the CAB, the ICC, and the FMC carry out a preliminary review to determine which actions require a more detailed analysis. For the most part, a substantive review occurs only when there appears to be a significant question about some economic or legal action in a case. In the same vein, the CPSC reviews products that might cause serious negative consequences if they were not regulated. In the SEC a branch chief makes a preliminary review of each case and then assigns the case to a subordinate for the appropriate detailed review. But the guidelines used by the branch chiefs are not published or otherwise available to an applicant. Neither the FCC nor the FDA has a review referral system.

The study demonstrates that the review referral systems that do exist are totally discretionary. The adoption of more-consistent screening techniques by federal agencies—particularly the ICC, the FMC, and the CAB—would reduce paperwork/information activity without reducing the regulatory effectiveness of the agencies.

General Petition Procedures

All regulatory agencies have procedures by which their decisions may be appealed. In establishing a proper petition process, the regulatees must have the right to offer legitimate protests, and the petition process must not inhibit timely and effective regulation.

In this study's examination of requests that came before the regulatory agencies, most were approved unquestionably. For example, 80 percent were approved by the ICC; 75 percent, by the FCC. There are, however, significant variations among agencies regarding the procedures that are to be used to challenge agency decisions. Most challenges to and revisions made by the SEC are informal; the agency's formal petition process is rarely used. In other agencies—such as the CAB, the FMC, the ICC, and the FCC—formal procedures—such as in-house reviews involving hearing examiners, administrative law judges, and commissioners as well as petitions to the federal courts—are used frequently.

Formal procedures are more information intensive and time consuming than informal procedures. The average prospectus can be revised and approved by the SEC within thirty to sixty days, but cases that come before the ICC or the FMC often take several years to be resolved. In fact, in cases handled by the ICC and the FMC, it is in the interest of an organization being challenged to delay proceedings since rates automatically take effect thirty days after being announced unless blocked by a suspension order. Even in the event of a suspension order, once the suspension period is over the rate goes into effect regardless of its legal status. Furthermore, no refund clause exists that would require a carrier to reimburse shippers if a new rate is eventually determined to be unlawful. On the other hand, the CAB presents an interesting contrast. Although the FMC and the ICC charters offer incentives to regulators (officials) to delay and draw out the petition process unnecessarily, the CAB

does not allow rates to go into effect until their legality is determined.

Determining what constitutes an appropriate petition process involves finding a middle ground between allowing the process to
stretch out for a long period of time and allowing the process to be
unnecessarily short so that relevant information cannot be taken
into account.

Review Staff Background

The professional background of a staff responsible for reviewing
applications and petitions significantly influences the nature of the
materials required for consideration, the method of review, and the
outcome of the review. In reality there is no such thing as "government regulation." There is only regulation by government officials.
As a result, the background of the regulators is a major factor in
determining the nature of the various regulatory processes. While
one can assume there is a correlation between the professional
background of a substantive rate-review staff and the types of
criteria used in making decisions on rate approval, it should be mentioned that review staffs have varying degrees of influence on rate
decisions. In an agency that does not give much decision authority
to the substantive review staff, the decision criteria may not directly reflect the professional background of that staff. This is the
case in the FMC where, despite financial and economic reviews,
rate decisions are ultimately based on negotiations and precedent.

Public Involvement

Although it would seem appropriate for the public to be involved
in the development of administrative rules, the case studies indicate
that the bulk of public involvement in rate matters occurs later during the rate approval process. Even then public involvement is
minimal because consumers are generally not sufficiently organized
to represent themselves before the commissioners.

Most agencies have endeavored to represent the consumer viewpoint during the rate approval process in one of two ways: by
allocating agency funds to pay for the appearance of consumer
representatives at rate approval proceedings or by creating an
agency unit to analyze rate proposals from the consumers' point of
view. The ICC, the CAB, and the FMC have all attempted the latter approach. Specifically, the CAB has a consumer advocate office,

which represents the consumer during rate approval proceedings. The ICC has a consumer unit in the tariff section that examines the impact of proposed rates on consumers and makes subsequent recommendations to the ICC for rate suspensions and/or investigations. The FMC has just created a consumer unit, but it is uncertain exactly what approach this unit will take.

Public involvement in the regulatory process results in high paperwork/information costs on the one hand and increased citizen wellbeing on the other. The most cost-effective method of ensuring public involvement would be to create a consumer advocate office within each agency since agency staffs are well acquainted with the subject matter dealt with by each agency and are thus able to bring more experience to bear on efforts to represent the consumer than the consumer himself is able to do.

Monitoring and Enforcement

Once standards have been set and agency decisions have been made, there is a continuing need to monitor activities and impose the appropriate penalties when violations occur. Significant variations exist among the agencies in monitoring techniques and the imposition of penalties, and the variations are the result of two philosophically different approaches: the preventative approach, which relies on intensive monitoring and inspection activities to reduce the chance of violations, and the punitive approach, which involves little continuous monitoring activity but imposes harsh penalties in the event of a violation. (Table 6.3 illustrates the contrasting approaches taken by the different agencies.)

The FDA and OSHA are examples of agencies that use the preventative approach. OSHA monitors factory practices on a continuing basis; in 1975 it conducted 81,000 work-place inspections in addition to requiring continual reports and recordkeeping by business firms. That same year, the FDA used one thousand consumer safety officers located throughout the United States to conduct 32,533 inspections and to make 37,079 sample analyses.

The ICC and the FMC are examples of agencies that use the punitive approach. Neither agency has the capacity to closely regulate all tariffs, but both are able to and do levy stiff penalties. For example, the FMC recently reached a $4 million settlement with a carrier that had violated agency regulations. A combination

Table 6.3

Monitoring and Enforcement

Agency	Preventative or Punitive or Process Feedback
ICC, CAB, FMC	Punitive
OSHA, FDA	Preventative
SEC, FCC	Punitive/Preventative
VA, SSA, CSC	Process Feedback

of both approaches also exists. The FCC conducted over 1,400 inspections and monitored 79,503 signals in 1976, but they also collected $168,301 in fines and initiated proceedings to revoke four licenses.

Monitoring can be used for purposes other than enforcement. This is the case in the CSC, the VA, and the SSA programs. Those agencies use monitoring data to generate aggregate statistics that help policymakers evaluate both how well employees use the rules and procedures and how adequate those rules and procedures are.

There is also considerable variation in the extent to which agencies use formal administrative procedures rather than informal negotiations. The SEC rarely uses its formal, internal petition process, relying predominantly upon informal negotiations. Although the ICC, the FMC, and the FCC make more use of their administrative procedures, they too resolve most conflicts through informal negotiations. Those agencies that do use formal administrative procedures to resolve most conflicts also vary considerably in the degree of reliance they place on internal remedies prior to going to the federal courts. Some agencies try to exhaust internal remedies before involving the courts. For example, the FDA relies on manufacturers to recall products voluntarily rather than on time-consuming and costly seizure orders from the court. The CSC, the VA, and the SSA will refrain from prosecuting cases of fraud if repayment is made, and they even charge no interest on the repayment. Other agencies will go to court. The CAB prefers to issue a court injunction rather than a cease-and-desist order because if an injunction is violated, a contempt-of-court citation can be brought immediately against the violator; if a cease-and-desist order is violated, the only course of redress is to ask the court for a preliminary injunction.

Court proceedings are extremely costly from a paperwork standpoint. They require detailed evidence. The EPA, the CPSC, and the SEC attorneys described the "discovery" process as well as the practices of gathering evidence for both sides as "asking for anything they might possibly need." If the government anticipates being taken to court, it will recommend the collection of as much background information (justification) as possible.

Several agencies have attempted to place greater personal responsibility on corporate officials for illegal corporate activities. The CAB, for example, can charge an airline official who has broken a regulation for the infraction and require him to appear in court on either a civil or criminal charge. Recently the SEC also has sought to place greater personal responsibility on specific corporate officials for illegal securities activities and has instituted a number of individual criminal proceedings.

In terms of paperwork/information, it is clear that low-monitoring procedures are less costly than high-monitoring ones. Furthermore, low monitoring combined with high penalties can be an effective deterrent. With the exception of the Consumer Product Safety Commission, all agencies examined require the submission of records and/or the maintenance of records on location as essential monitoring devices. These requirements obviously result in a great amount of paperwork. Alternatives, such as random site visits, the use of existing data sources, tipoffs, and complaints, are also used. However, about half of the agencies describe these alternatives as being in addition to, rather than a replacement for, "paper" monitoring. The alternative techniques alone would clearly cost less in terms of paperwork/information than filing reports.

Informal procedures are less costly than formal procedures. When agencies can work out informal agreements with regulated parties, the paper flow is diminished and staff time is released for other work. Assuming that such agreements are conducted in an open forum to ensure that the public interest is fairly represented, such methods should be encouraged.

7

Comparative Administrative Practices: Three Case Studies

For the reader interested in the details of the comparative studies that were performed, the three studies in the area of regulatory activities are presented in this chapter. The comparative study in the area of service delivery activities is not presented because of time and space limitations.

THE EPA, OSHA, AND THE CPSC

This study examines three federal agencies that regulate health and safety activities in the public interest. They are (1) the Environmental Protection Agency, responsible for the quality of air and water;[1] (2) the Occupational Safety and Health Administration, responsible for safety and health standards in industrial plants; and (3) the Consumer Product Safety Commission, responsible for the health and safety standards for consumer products. The major form of regulatory activity undertaken by these three federal agencies is the establishment, monitoring, and enforcement of national standards for industry and the public.

Standards Development

There are various ways in which standards can be developed. One extreme is to define problem areas and write standards within the agency; the other extreme is to have problem areas defined and written by outside groups with near-automatic government approval. Between these two extremes there are a variety of specific practices that will affect the paperwork burden and the associated information costs. We hypothesize that three specific practices would be valuable in terms of information efficiency.

1. A clear definition of the problem requiring regulation and an initial setting of priorities should result in fewer information requirements.
2. Giving respondents and other interested parties a chance to comment on and participate in the development of regulations should result in less-burdensome information requirements without affecting standards.
3. Specific practices such as providing better indexes to agency files and clearly defined statements of proposed information use should result in lowered respondent burden and increase agency effectiveness.

Evidence to support all these contentions was found in the three agencies studied.

Problem Definition

Problem definition is the first step in the development of standards. The CPSC has the most explicit definition of problems and the clearest establishment of priorities of the three agencies reviewed. It uses the National Electronic Injury and Surveillance System (NEISS),[2] form petitions to the commission, other government agency data systems (e.g., that of the National Center for Health Statistics), and hotline calls and letters to determine problems. Once problems are identified, the commission selects items for priority attention. This priority system weighs the risks and hazards associated with a product against other factors including economic considerations, the need for standards, and probable impact.

The EPA has a congressional mandate, which is clear: to improve air and water quality. Problem definition consists of determining the types of pollutants to be regulated and the allowable pollution levels. To define the problem and set priorities, the EPA uses agency-sponsored and other research, National Academy of Sciences reports, scientific literature, results of water- and air-quality monitoring, and public comment.

OSHA was found to have the least effective definition of

priorities. Initially the agency adopted the guidelines of the American National Standards Institute to define problems and establish priorities. Now it is developing "permanent" standards by using data from the Bureau of Labor Statistics, workers' compensation data, OSHA inspection-file data, industry and academic literature, and public comment.

Writing of Standards

The second step in the development of standards is the actual writing of the standards. The Consumer Product Safety Commission has the most effective practice, "the offerer process," which involves respondents and interested parties in the standard-setting process. This practice, which is mandatory under the Consumer Product Safety Act and optional under the other four acts that the CPSC enforces, invites the public—both consumer groups and industry—to write standards for particular products in which they have an interest. These standards are then reviewed by the agency and after public comment and revision are referred to the commissioners for adoption. In short, interested participants develop the initial standards with government review, rather than the government developing the standards first with public comment and review coming later. This "offerer process" has been used for the development of seven out of approximately forty standards that have been developed since the CPSC came into existence. The EPA also has an explicit approach to public participation in standard setting that appears effective. Standards are developed in-house, with provision for public comment and participation.

At least initially, OSHA had no public participation in the setting of standards. It took the "guidelines" of the American National Standards Institute (ANSI) and turned them into "interim standards." Those guidelines are models of plant safety standards that were developed through industry consensus. Although they are called "interim," the majority are still in effect, but permanent standards are being developed by OSHA and public participation and comment will be requested.

The 1946 Administrative Procedures Act requires that government agencies request public comment and participation in the formulation of new regulations. In addition to this general requirement, some federal agencies have specific policies to encourage public participation. The EPA, for example, requires that there be a plan for public participation when new regulations are established. On October 17, 1976, the CPSC released product profiles on thirty-five consumer products, summarizing the available data and the analysis developed by the agency for each product. Through such publications the public is informed on how decisions are made in the agency, what information is available, and how it is used.

Nature and Coverage of Standards

There are three types of standards: national/objective, process, and performance. One extreme on the spectrum of standards consists of overall objective standards that establish broad, quantifiable priorities based on scientific analyses and value judgments. These standards regulate performance at the general level and do not address specific concerns. The other extreme on the spectrum consists of process standards that specify input and design features based on engineering data of good performance technology. These standards regulate specific concerns. Between the extremes lie performance standards, which specify performance or output levels of a particular plant or product.

The coverage of standards is comprehensive or selective. Comprehensive coverage includes all possible violators; selective coverage focuses on specific types or categories of potential violators. The former should be used in cases when considerations of equity and single violations are important; the latter (the more cost-effective method) should be used when equity and single violations are not of primary concern.

The type of standard and its coverage have varying implications for the effectiveness and the efficiency of a program, particularly for the reporting burden placed on the private sector. With reference to these implications, we hypothesize the following:

1. The practice of translating objectives into quantifiable, general standards is likely to improve the effectiveness of a program in attaining its objectives.
2. Because performance standards regulate ends, not means, they are a more direct method of achieving program objectives than are process standards, which regulate means. Furthermore, performance standards encourage technological ad-

vances whereas process standards tend to limit such advances.

3. The selective approach to standards coverage has the greatest potential for the least cost but sacrifices considerations of equity and the seriousness of single violations.

The nature of the standards employed varies from one federal agency to another. The EPA uses several types to maximize the probability of achieving its overall program objectives. First, the EPA developed national air- and water-quality standards that defined the amount of pollution allowable. Then it translated those national objectives into performance standards that specify emission limitation levels. By 1983, these objectives may also be translated into some process specifications (input or design standards).

In contrast, OSHA has only process standards that regulate the input and design features of plants and equipment. It does not develop overall objective standards, nor standards that quantify OSHA national priorities in terms of the reduction of occupational illness and injury. There are not even any performance standards to regulate the results of plant or equipment operations on worker safety and health. The CPSC sets product standards based on performance and process, roughly half of which are mandatory, but the agency does not quantify its national objectives into specific standards.

The coverage of standards also varies significantly among the federal agencies. The EPA standards apply to all actual or potential stationary polluters, and in OSHA standards apply to all work places having one or more employees. In contrast, the CPSC standards are selective in their coverage. That agency has two basic approaches to such selectivity: the first is coverage of products demonstrating the highest hazard incidence, and the second is reactive coverage, that is, coverage of potentially hazardous products that are brought to the attention of the CPSC by the public.

Implementation of Standards

There are two important considerations in comparing the implementation of standards in different federal agencies: bureaucratic organization and procedural technique. We hypothesized that (1) standards implementation entails a greater relative burden on small businesses than on large ones; (2) decentralization results in a complex system of administration, which increases the potential for inefficiency and mismanagement; and (3) permit issuance is a time- and resource-consuming process, which results in extensive paperwork.

Administrative Structure

The implementation of EPA programs is delegated to states in the form of state plans (air) and permits (water), although regions maintain authority for states lacking sufficient resources and management capability. State authority is circumscribed, however, by the need to attain national air- and water-quality objective standards.

Similarly, OSHA delegates implementation authority to those states that demonstrate sufficient resource and management capabilities. Even the authority to develop standards is delegated to the states that exhibit those capabilities. In those cases, state authority is circumscribed only if OSHA rescinds the state's previous authority, a rare event.

On the other hand, the CPSC retains the principal administrative authority on both the federal and the regional levels. Some states are responsible for enforcing federal standards, and a few states are in the process of legislating their own standards, which will be consistent with the federal statutes.

As the section on monitoring techniques indicates, the EPA/OSHA reporting burden is substantially larger than that of the CPSC. Moreover, the extensive reporting requirements at various levels of government support the hypothesis that decentralization results in management problems.

Procedural Techniques

Procedurally, all three agencies implement their programs in a similar manner. Standards are set for product or industry/source categories, and the standards are enforced by monitoring and penalties. In addition, the EPA uses a permit process. Rather than simply requiring that all sources within a particular category achieve the specified emission limitation set for that category, the permit process tailors the limitation standards to suit the unique characteristics of each individual polluting source. Thus, the permit enables the individual sources to better understand and achieve the standards. The permit also sets forth the monitoring and inspection requirements.

Monitoring Techniques

Significant differences exist among the three agencies in terms of the content and information burden of their monitoring systems. The CPSC has no formal reporting techniques and no defined set of consumer products over which it has jurisdiction. It monitors regulation compliance through site visits and programs, and most data are collected from treatment sources, e.g., emergency rooms, doctors' offices, hospitals, and clinics. Both the EPA and OSHA are more comprehensive in their regulatory requirements. The former monitors all air and water polluters; the latter monitors all industries with seven or more workers.

We hypothesize that on the federal level

1. reports and recordkeeping would be a more costly monitoring approach than site visits and acting on complaints.
2. agencies with extensive records would be more effective in their overall monitoring techniques.
3. agencies that gathered information from complaints would be more effective in enforcement performance and have a greater receptivity of enforcement practices by the public.
4. agencies function most effectively when their jurisdictional boundaries are well defined.
5. well-planned field visits would increase the efficiency of the regulatory agency and of the concerned industry.

The EPA has the most extensive monitoring system, requiring industries to file reports in three main areas. First, compliance schedules, summarizing progress toward the completion of construction of pollution control systems, are usually submitted biannually. Second, reports on monitoring tests, data, and analysis are required annually, except for major polluters who must report more frequently, sometimes on a monthly or quarterly basis. Third, notification of excessive emission and of new, potential air polluting sources are required whenever they occur. Additionally, the EPA water and air programs require industry to maintain records of emission data obtained by frequent self-monitoring. OSHA requires that industry submit reports about any occupational injury or illness and maintain records demonstrating compliance with most standards.

The CPSC, unlike the EPA and OSHA, does not require that the industries it monitors write formal reports regarding the actions they have taken or propose to take in order to comply with CPSC rulings. Informal reports describing the progress of a firm or industry in correcting a particular violative action are exchanged between federal and regional offices, but they do not appear to be used. Additional information is gathered from the general public and industry by means of surveys, questionnaires, and solicited and unsolicited comments. The highly successful consumer deputy program is a part of the agency's overall surveillance activities. It solicits volunteer workers (general consumers) to conduct door-to-door surveys—using a questionnaire geared to the product under investigation—as well as to keep a watch on retail stores. These data provide a comprehensive picture of compliance by a specific industry and the names of specific companies that comply or do not comply with the standards, and, finally, the publicity that promotes the program encourages self-initiated compliance within the industry.

All three federal agencies conduct field inspections and/or site visits to monitor compliance, but in varying degrees. The CPSC depends primarily upon its site visits to document compliance with or violation of any aspect of the five statutes administered by the commission, OSHA uses site visits and reporting equally, and the EPA primarily uses reporting.

Approximately one-hundred fifty investigators in thirteen CPSC area offices conducted more than fifty-two hundred site visits in 1975. Typically, a site inspector gathers data that describe those people responsible for each part of the firm's operations, reviews the firm's complaint files to judge where problem areas exist, assesses any product guarantee(s) that exist, evaluates products for their compliance to regulations, and checks the firm's quality control program and the components/raw materials the firm uses in production. The inspector examines the firm's product coding and distribution systems (including the recall system and shipping data) and collects information about promotion and advertising methods and the record-keeping system.

The major obstacle to using CPSC site visits as a monitoring technique is the lack of premarket clearance provisions. It is not mandatory for the manufacturers who are subject to CPSC standards and regulations to register with the commission; rather the agency is responsible for identifying potentially dangerous products and applying agency standards and other requirements to them.

OSHA also uses site visits extensively to guarantee compliance with health and safety standards. In 1975, for example, it sent eleven hundred inspectors from sixty-four area offices to conduct eighty-one thousand inspections. During such visits, evidence from witnesses and testimony under oath are required to support the inspector's report. Subsequent to the inspection, offenders receive citations stating which regulation has been violated, and they are given a reasonable amount of time, known as the abatement period, to remedy the situation.

All three agencies also have a mechanism to handle the reporting and investigating of citizen/worker/consumer complaints. The EPA, for example, asks citizens who notice evidence of air pollution to contact the local air-pollution-control agency that has direct jurisdiction. Evidence of water pollution is reported to the state or local agency or, for major offenders, to the National Enforcement Division. In all cases, citizen complaints result in some inspection or check by the EPA or other agencies under its jurisdictions. Similarly, workers who observe unsafe conditions in a work place are asked to notify the regional OSHA office. All such complaints result in an OSHA inspection.

Since there is no one system that can collect data on all product-related injuries and deaths, the CPSC receives consumer complaints from many sources, the most useful of which is treatment centers. The National Electronic Injury Surveillance System gathers injury data from a statistical sample of hospital emergency rooms, and states provide death certificates identifying product-related deaths. Product-injury data are collected through the National Health Interview Survey and the National Ambulatory Medical Care Survey (a survey of physicians' offices). In addition, the agency has an Injury Surveillance Desk that collects, reviews, and classifies information on product-related injuries and potentially hazardous products reported by non-NEISS sources. The non-NEISS sources include consumer complaint correspondence; hotline calls; news media articles; referrals from federal, state, and local government agencies;

and reports from consumer groups, fire departments, school and college sports events, and the National Injury Information Clearinghouse. In 1975, accidents reported within the commission's jurisdiction numbered 6,688, of which 54 percent involved injuries.

Paperwork may possibly be reduced if OSHA, the EPA, and the CPSC share information with any outside agencies and/or private groups that may have need of the same information. Also, computerizing this information, as the CPSC did with NEISS, simplifies the retrieval of information.

Enforcement of Standards

To ensure compliance with standards, informal and formal administrative remedies and judicial procedures are used. The former include letters, phone calls, publicity, orders, and administrative fines; the latter usually result in injunctions that require corrective action and impose civil penalties. Criminal penalties are infrequently imposed and, when they are, they usually result in fines, rarely imprisonment.

To enforce agency standards, we found that

1. agencies use a variety of informal approaches including letters, informative phone calls, and technical assistance to gain compliance with standards before attempting formal enforcement actions.
2. judicial procedures are used as a last resort.
3. adequate monitoring and the threat of effective sanctions are required to strengthen voluntary compliance efforts.
4. informal negotiations are the least costly in information and time delays, court procedures are the most costly, and the costs of administrative enforcement are between the two.
5. a system of self-monitoring backed up by the threat of the imposition of severe penalties for violations is the least costly approach in terms of resource input and reporting burden placed on the private sector.
6. when information efforts associated with enforcement are costly, reliance is placed on few actions and high penalties; when the necessary information efforts are less costly, there are more frequent actions and lower penalties.

Use of Informal Methods

Interviews with the EPA and the CPSC documented that these agencies emphasize informal methods to ensure compliance with regulations, although when compliance is forthcoming they use sanctions as implied threats. In contrast, OSHA concentrates its enforcement activities on citing and penalizing offending companies.

The informal methods used by the EPA and the CPSC attempt to inform, assist, and negotiate with the actual and potential violators and to persuade them to comply with the regulations. The enforcement orders they issue often recognize that the violator is ready to comply, and a case is closed when compliance occurs. In OSHA, however, there are unannounced inspections by a compliance officer, and the regional offices always issue citations to any company or industry that violates any aspect of the Occupational Safety and Health Act. There is some flexibility in compliance timing; the abatement period, which allows a violator time to meet all the standards, may be adjusted.

Surprisingly, the informal negotiations of the EPA and the CPSC do not appear to be more efficient or less costly in terms of information and time delays than the administrative fine procedures of OSHA or the state EPA offices. However, the use of informal techniques such as letters, site visits, and negotiations result in less paperwork if their use keeps the agency and affected parties out of the courts and can be carried out without the need for any formal monitoring systems.

Administrative Enforcement

Formal administrative remedies are rarely used in the EPA and the CPSC until after informal techniques prove unsatisfactory. In the EPA, enforcement programs include administrative consent and emergency orders. A few states—such as Connecticut, Illinois, and Pennsylvania—also have the power to levy monetary penalties for noncompliance. This power provides an intermediate enforcement option between issuing an order and referring a case to the courts for judicial action, which is useful given the cost, time, and paperwork involved in litigation.

Of the three agencies examined, OSHA uses administrative penalties most extensively, directly, and severely. Primarily it fines violators of agency regulations. As a result of site inspections in

1975, 367,778 violations were cited, and they resulted in
$12,449,706 in penalties. Repeated violators face civil penalty fines
not to exceed $10,000, and employers who fail to amend a violation
within the abatement period are liable to a fine of $1,000 a day as
long as the violation continues. (The average penalty in 1975 for a
serious violation was $600; for a nonserious violation, $20.)
Businesses that refuse to correct violations risk judicial action.

The use of fines as an enforcement strategy has the potential of
reducing the amount of information required, collected, and used.
Although fines do not eliminate monitoring information requirements, they have a strong deterrent effect without the cost in
time and information of litigation.

Judicial Enforcement

All three of the agencies have judicial enforcement powers, but
because of the extreme cost they use them only as a last resort.
They can employ several judicial enforcement techniques including
civil and criminal penalties and injunctions. In 1976 for example, the
CPSC imposed the following penalties: two injunctions, six criminal
prosecutions, fifteen product seizures, and two access orders. The
agency also assumed, upon its establishment, responsibility for enforcing 150 cease-and-desist orders initiated by the Federal Trade
Commission. The Occupational Safety and Health Review Commission processed 4,896 administrative, not judicial, cases in fiscal year
1976. OSHA officials reported that the number of judicial proceedings was significantly lower than the number of cases heard by
the review commission, but they were unable to indicate the exact
figure. (These figures and estimates represent cases from those
states in which OSHA has sole jurisdiction and exclude cases in
states that have undertaken enforcement of all OSHA regulations in
accordance with state-approved plans.)

The information costs associated with judicial proceedings result
from the amount of information required when attempting to prosecute violators and from the judicial review of standards development. The amount of information that attorneys require from
government and the other litigants is voluminous. A CPSC attorney
stated that the tendency is for both sides to ask for everything they
can think of, just to be sure. Plaintiffs in pollution cases are like
plaintiffs in any other: they have burdens of proof to meet. Pros-

ecutors attempt to minimize the risk of loss by encouraging their client agencies to supply evidence that is more than sufficient to prove violation, but gathering such evidence can be an expensive undertaking.

Moreover, in the case of a judicial review of standards, the results of litigation can be court-ordered requirements that direct an agency to document its case for a standard more thoroughly, i.e., provide more information. Such a court decision resulted in a major new survey of industry carried out by the EPA. The appeals process, which in theory increases the probability of equitable treatment, can result in further information costs.

In short, litigation is time consuming, complex, expensive, unpredictable, and heavily paperwork intensive. Regulatory agencies must decide whether a case is important enough to prosecute. Then they have to persuade an attorney general or a U.S. attorney that the case is worth the time it will require, as well as the expense of litigation. Litigation, therefore, is usually used sparingly and for the more serious violations.

THE FCC, THE FDA, AND THE SEC

This study examines three federal agencies that engage in prior approval of private sector activities. The three agencies and corresponding approval activities are (1) the Federal Communications Commission, which approves new radio and television broadcasting facilities; (2) the Food and Drug Administration, which approves food and color additives; and (3) the Securities and Exchange Commission, which approves security registration statements.[3]

The same comparative framework used previously is used here to contrast the approval procedures of these three agencies. Similarly, attention is focused on what their administrative practices reveal about managing information/paperwork activities with a view toward suggesting more efficient and effective management procedures. It should be noted that unlike the preceding sections on comparative administrative practices that contrasted identical substantive topics (e.g., rate making or medical eligibility), this study compares three agencies that must perform the same procedural function—prior approval—in three unrelated and diverse substantive areas. Consequently more detailed descriptive material on the practices of the three agencies is presented in order to adequately understand the comparisons and comments. It should be noted further that the degree of injury to the public that results from inadequate procedures by these three agencies varies greatly. For example, inadequate approval procedures in the area of food additives may result in grave injury to the whole population while inadequate approval procedures in the area of radio broadcasting may affect only a small number of people in a fairly minor way. As a result, administrative practices that are appropriate for the FDA may be unnecessary for the FCC, and may in fact be unjustified in light of a potential adverse effect on the public. It is important for the reader to bear this difference in mind when drawing conclusions as to the merits of the various administrative practices and procedures used by these three agencies.

Standards Development

Specificity of Legislation

With the exception of the Delaney Amendment, all three agencies are forced to establish regulatory operations based on general and imprecise legislative language, which causes unique problems for each agency. The congressional legislation giving the FCC approval of broadcasting facilities and the legislation giving the SEC approval of registration statements represent one extreme in legislative drafting; the legislation giving the FDA approval of food and color additives represents the other. The FCC and the SEC legislation are characterized by a lack of articulated standards, but the FDA legislation is unduly specific in the area of food and color additives.

The FCC, for example, approves and grants broadcasting licenses and regulates broadcasting in "the public interest, convenience and necessity." No specific legislative guidelines or criteria for granting licenses are expounded. As a result, conflicts over the meaning of "the public interest" are recurrent. Besides lending itself to various interpretations, the vague statutory mandate has hampered the development of coherent public policy since Congress can and often does declare, "That is not what we mean by the public interest." Vagueness about what power is delegated often has served to limit the agency's independence and freedom of action rather than encouraging them.

The SEC legislation follows a similar vein, providing only that the registration statement must be an "adequate and accurate" disclosure of facts concerning the company and the securities it proposes to sell. Both "adequate" and "accurate" are highly subjective standards. What appears to be a standard can be too easily reduced to a debate over writing styles and the number of visual aid charts to be included in the disclosure materials.

At the other extreme lies the legislation for the approval of food and color additives, the Delaney Amendment. In order to determine whether a food or color additive is safe, the FDA has been saddled with a standard that is so specific that it allows no administrative flexibility and leaves the agency open to public ridicule. By congressional mandate, "no additive shall be deemed to be safe if it is found to induce cancer when ingested by man or animal." If laboratory experiments verify that a substance produces a cancer in animals, the substance cannot be approved for use! The fact that the quantity of the substance necessary to produce that cancer means that a human being must drink over eight hundred cans a day for twenty years of some liquid containing the carcinogenic substance, and the fact that such a person would clearly die of a ruptured bladder or some other physical malfunction long before any cancer would develop are irrelevant. If it can be positively demonstrated by an applicant that an additive is noncarcinogenic, then the congressional mandate for approval is that the additive be "safe" for human consumption and "effective" for the purpose intended.

This is clearly an example of legislative overkill. Although clarity makes possible more rigorous and objective decision making, there is a danger in being so specific that one ends up with an inappropriate decision that the public will not accept as valid and within its interest. A precise standard must also be a realistic standard that permits flexibility.

In summary, inadequate or inappropriate legislation has hampered the efficiency and effectiveness of the three agencies from the outset. Vague and unrealistic legislative mandates are a root cause of excessive information/paperwork activities. When standards are vague, administrative officials have broad discretion, which allows, if not breeds, intensive lobbying efforts by private parties and associations. Voluminous information is submitted to officials to assist and influence them in rendering a favorable decision. If this approach fails, members of Congress are approached; this tactic is used especially with respect to the FCC as the strong influence the Senate Commerce Committee has had on the activities of that agency demonstrates. Vague and inappropriate legislative standards also become the grounds for a proliferation of costly, time-consuming, and paperwork-intensive court actions. "Due process" and "equal protection" issues are readily put forward; even worse, suits based on claims of vague, inadequate, and inappropriate administrative standards often lead to judicial standard writing rather than to congressional legislative writing. Since federal judges are appointed, not elected, this seems potentially dangerous for a representative democracy.

Nature of Standards and Rules

All three agencies have varying degrees of the three types of standards generally used by agencies: national objectives, performance standards (output), and process standards (input). Each of the three agencies has been given a broad legislative mandate that represents a national objective directed toward enhancing citizen well-being. With the exception of the FDA, these broad standards have proved meaningless in augmenting and accomplishing the national objectives. Consequently, each agency relies on one or both of the other types of standards in carrying out the approval process.

The FDA and the FCC (more recently) are primarily output oriented. In essence, they will let an applicant determine and propose a "package" that meets the agency's objectives and public responsibility. For example, at the FDA an applicant must submit data to prove the safety and effectiveness of a product, placing the ultimate responsibility for safety on the manufacturer. The FDA, however, does set the tolerance limitation on the exact amount of the food or color additive permissible in a product to assure its safety, and the agency also works with manufacturers to develop and establish good manufacturing practices.

At the FCC, the burden is also on the applicant to present an application that demonstrates an intention to not interfere with another radio signal, explains what the public need is, and shows how that need will be met. Since 1972, the FCC has had a Re-

regulation Task Force to revise and simplify rules that pertain mainly to radio broadcasting. The purpose was to reduce the workload and paperwork of those regulated. During the first four years of its existence, every rule relating to radio broadcasting was scrutinized, and over five hundred rules were revised, modified, or deleted. In general, there has been a tendency toward lessening the strict input-type standards in favor of less time-consuming output requirements.

In short, both the FDA and the FCC are passive agencies. They sit back, accept applications, and let the applicants demonstrate why it is in the public interest to permit them to do what they are requesting. The focus is more on the end product desired and less on having complex rules and procedures to achieve that end.

The SEC takes a more active role than the other two agencies, and it is input oriented. While it pays lip service to the notion that the burden of full disclosure is on the registrant and that legally it remains there in the event of prosecution, in reality the agency dictates the manner and content of the registration statement instead of just reviewing it for accuracy and completeness. The agency specifies the exact type of financial and other corporate data that must appear in the prospectus, how it is to be written and arranged, and virtually the size type it must appear in.

For administrative convenience, however, a modified form of output standard is used by the SEC in over 25 percent of the applications. A registration statement may be given a "cursory" review or a "summary" review. In such instances, letters are required from the chief executive of the company, accountants, and managing underwriters on behalf of all underwriters stating that all are aware that only a limited review has been made of the registration statement and that they are aware of their statutory responsibility to provide full and honest disclosure. (This practice will be discussed in greater detail in the section on intensity of review.)

In terms of effectiveness and paperwork/information, the approach used by the FCC and the FDA appears more efficient than that of the SEC for the following reasons: (1) the majority of the SEC standards are input standards, (2) 95 percent of all registration statements are changed by the SEC staff, and (3) over 50 percent of SEC staff time is spent on enforcement activities. In addition to the advantage of efficiency, output standards permit greater individual flexibility and creativity within the context of public responsibility without an apparent loss in regulatory effectiveness.

Coverage of Standards

There are two basic approaches toward the coverage of regulatory rules, comprehensive and selective. The FCC and the FDA coverage is total, and the SEC coverage is subject to specific legislative exemptions. With respect to the FCC, prior approval must be granted before the construction and operation of all broadcasting facilities. Similarly, the FDA must give premarket approval to all food and color additives.[4] Although the SEC registration requirement applies to securities of both domestic and foreign private issuers as well as to securities of foreign governments or their agents, there are certain exemptions from the registration requirements.[5]

In 1976, the FCC received 3,023 applications for new stations, 1,613 requests for major changes in an existing station, and 9,511 renewal requests.[6] The total number of man-years expended for authorization of service was 181.2 at a cost of $3,151,599. That same year, the FDA received 90 petitions for approval of food and color additives. The total number of man-years expended in the approval process was 106.3 at a cost of $6,129,916.[7] In 1975, the SEC received 2,365 new applications and 3,866 posteffective amendments. The number of man-years expended in reviewing and approving the applications was 55.7.[8] As already indicated, the SEC, unlike the FCC and the FDA, utilizes a preliminary substantive review process to determine the intensity of review an application will receive. Numerous types of securities offered would cause little attendant injury to the public in the event of fraud or misrepresentation. Thus, although it is appropriate from an information/paperwork point of view for the SEC to seek ways to concentrate its review activities on those cases that might cause the greatest harm, such a procedure would seem less appropriate for the FCC and the FDA. This does not mean, however, that those agencies should not try to find the most efficient and effective methods for reviewing all applications.

Rationale of Standards

Since congressional legislation that establishes the approval process for each of the three agencies is based on general objectives open to broad discretionary interpretations, with noted exceptions each agency must formulate appropriate standards. Thus, it is important to determine whether the standards are clear, predictable, and equitable, and thus presumably less paperwork intensive, or whether the approval process is largely discretionary, which casts an aura of unpredictability and uncertainty over judgments and promotes and increases paperwork activity.

Although the FDA appears to be able to exercise the least amount of discretion of the three agencies, it also possesses the greatest power to inflict harm on the public if its judgments are erroneous. Standards are shrouded in analytic laboratory data, but the determination of the type, number, and extent of the tests required of an applicant to prove product safety is judgmental. Recent congressional investigation disclosing the harassment of FDA scientists thought by agency officials to be anti-industry shows the effect individual attitudes can have on the approval process. Attempts to "neutralize" staff members through exile to undesirable posts are another example of individual idiosyncrasies to which the approval process is vulnerable.

Before discussing the approval process at the FCC, it is necessary to point out that there are only so many frequencies (AM) and channels (FM) to be assigned. That commission, unlike the SEC and the FDA, is dealing with a limited commodity; there is much competition, and there can be only a few winners.

In applying to the FCC for a signal, an applicant must first demonstrate and then have verified that he can maintain the integrity of the signal and prevent interference with other signals. Assuming that several applicants can demonstrate this capability, the commission must then determine which applicant will best serve "the public interest." A number of standards are published in order to reduce the amount of discretion used in making such a determination. Among the rules are the following limitations on the ownership of broadcasting facilities: (1) an individual or company cannot own more than seven AM, seven FM, and seven TV stations (no more than five of which can be VHF), (2) no one can operate two commercial stations of the same type covering the same geographic area, and (3) no licensee can be the owner of a daily newspaper in the same market. If two or more applicants overcome these hurdles and meet the technical and financial requirements,[9] then approval becomes a matter of discretion on the part of the FCC. Although certain policy criteria have been formulated over the years that favor local ownership and operation over absentee ownership and management, in the end the commission must decide which applicant can best satisfy a community's interests and needs.

The FCC's inability to formulate more decisive and substantive guidelines for the awarding of radio and TV licenses has resulted in constant congressional and industrial pressures and in judicial reversal. The commission often substitutes the act of evaluating and studying a problem for the act of formulating policy criteria. The result is administrative chaos and increased paperwork activity.

Approval by the SEC is extremely judgmental from start to finish, and the type of additional information required after initial filing, the degree of review made, and the changes demanded vary. Many of the judgments become formalized within the corporate finance branch for administrative convenience, but the applicant is still very much at the mercy and opinion of the reviewing attorney, the financial analysts, and the particular branch chief assigned to review the application.

This discretionary latitude is subject to an interesting parallel force, personal contact. Once a corporation has been assigned to one of the fifteen reviewing branches through a purely random process, all future registration applications by that corporation are reviewed by the same branch. Since civil servants tend to remain ensconced in their bureaucratic niches, close professional ties may arise between a regulator and those he regulates. What begins as a discretionary review can easily grow into a friendly alliance. Thus, although 95 percent of the applications are changed before they become effective, an application is rarely reviewed again once the changes are requested; the SEC staff assumes that the changes will be made by the applicant. Mutual trust rather than precise rules underlies the entire process.

Generally, the predominant use of informal practices over the use of cumbersome, costly, and time-consuming formal methods is laudable in respect to paperwork, but the informal practices of the SEC are hardly laudable from the viewpoint of fairness and equity or, in the end, paperwork efficiency. Because the SEC standards are so loose, corporations submit materials that cast them in the best light and sit back waiting for the SEC to request more. Assuming that the application is not so patently defective that it is rejected at the preliminary review stage, the company can easily submit more information and countless amendments. Too often corporations submit inadequate registration statements in order to "get in line" and expect staff comments to provide the necessary incentive for submitting the requisite material for compliance. A process that is so discretionary to begin with, coupled with the informal nature of the dealings between the corporations and the SEC staff, is not likely to ensure that the public is being best served and protected.

An alternative approach might be to close off this informal process at some point and require a hearing if the information submitted is grossly inadequate or biased. The mere threat of a public hearing, with the attendant public notice of the conflict between a corporation and the SEC, might be an effective, inexpensive administrative tool to secure initial compliance and thus reduce needless staff and paperwork burdens.

It can be said that all three agencies are a prime illustration of the fact that imprecise congressional legislation usually results in imprecise administrative rules, which, in turn, lead to ambiguity and the exercise of discretion on the part of the decision makers. Ambiguous rules lead to multiple interpretations, none of which can be definitely proved to be correct. The result is a high paperwork-intensive situation.

Standards Implementation

Petition Process

The formal petition process in each agency, with one exception that will be discussed later, is fundamentally the same. Substantive differences, if any, are not readily determinable and arise primarily from the practical operation of the system. In general, there are about six key decision points in the petition process. There is a preliminary procedural review by a nontechnical staff member to ensure that the application is apparently complete. Notice of receipt is then made public in the *Federal Register*. The application is then sent to another division for technical and substantive staff review and for comments and recommendations that are then communicated to the applicant. An approval memorandum is written and signed by one or two levels of division and bureau chiefs. It is then sent to the commissioners or an assistant director for approval.

A noticeable variation in this process is the frequent information feedback exchanges between SEC personnel and an applicant. The SEC procedure requires a review of staff comments and recommendations by the branch chief and the transmittal of the comments and recommended changes to the applicant. The applicant then makes the recommended changes[10] and returns the statement to the branch office for additional review. If there are no further comments or recommendations, this fact is communicated to the applicant, and the applicant then usually requests an acceleration of the effective date. This request is reviewed by the branch staff, and the decision is communicated to the applicant. If acceleration is granted, a memo stating approval of the registration statement is prepared and signed by the assistant director on behalf of the commission. At this point, the applicant receives formal notice of approval and may offer the securities for purchase.

The most important difference in management practices among the agencies is the time the whole process takes. By statute, the SEC must complete its review in twenty days and the FDA in ninety days from the date of acceptance of the application. Approval is rarely accomplished within the statutory period. The law provides for an extension for good cause, and an agency can begin the timing of the process anew if additional information is requested and submitted. Applicants rarely protest time delays for fear of further delay, additional paperwork, or an adverse decision.

Less than 1 percent of the applications received by the SEC and the FDA require an administrative hearing, but 25 percent of the new broadcasting applications require a hearing. From a paperwork and man-hour standpoint, the low percentage requiring a hearing is important and would be commendable if it were the result of an efficient approval process resulting from the application of clear and concise standards. Unfortunately this is not the case. With respect to the SEC, a hearing would entail publicity, and any publicity concerning the securities of a company and a disagreement with the SEC would probably affect adversely the sale of those securities. Consequently, regardless of the merits of their case, most companies will generally avoid a public hearing. With respect to the FDA, hearings are extremely costly and can delay the petition process for years. In both instances, compromise is more prudent although not necessarily more beneficial to the public interest.

Clarity

All three agencies have published their rules and procedures regarding submission and information requirements. But the important questions of how this information will be used and what criteria will be applied in making an evaluation are, for the most part, not answered, which results in the exercise of broad discretion in the approval process. Discretion means ambiguity, and ambiguity means that many unnecessary requests are made in the hope of getting approval and, therefore, unnecessary paperwork is generated.

The FCC offers the best information on what criteria are applied in considering an application. An applicant is given a simple, easily read information bulletin on how to apply for a broadcast license. Along with the standardized forty-two-page application form, the commission also provides the applicant with the same checklist agency engineers will use in evaluating and checking the information. Since the institution of the Re-regulation Task Force, pertinent policy statements and requirements associated with various agency forms are appropriately documented in the rules of procedure. Lastly, the FCC provides a telephone directory that lists the appropriate departments, personnel, and phone numbers to call for information and assistance. Still, to fill out the application form as accurately as possible, the applicant must employ expert engineering and legal services.

In contrast, applicants to the SEC and the FDA are never quite sure what information is required or how the information is used and evaluated before approval is granted or denied. The general SEC registration form is thirty-nine pages long with a separate thirty-nine-page publication guide. To facilitate the registration of securities by different types of issuers, the commission has, however, adopted several short forms that vary in their disclosure requirements so that there can be a maximum disclosure of the essential facts pertinent for a given type of offering while at the same time the burden and expense of compliance with the law can be minimized. From time to time the commission publishes guidelines that reflect current policies and practices followed by the Corporate Finance Division in the administration of the registration requirements, but not policy guidelines on how the submitted information will be evaluated.

At the FDA, there are still significant gaps concerning what data tests are necessary to fulfill the formal petition requirements. Any item proposed for direct addition to food or for food contact (i.e., an indirect food additive) must undergo testing to establish the safety of the intended use. The FDA has developed "Guidelines for Chemistry and Technology Requirements of Food Additive Petitions and others for indirect food additives, but according to agency officials no guidelines are possible in the area of toxicology.

To keep the FDA petition system from remaining a total mystery, agency officials maintain a continuing dialogue with the twenty major firms that account for 65 percent of the food-and-color-additive petitions and with any other firms wishing to avail themselves of the informal information system. Agency officials also hold two or three conferences a week with firms seeking clarification of petition data. Although these procedures offer a means of reducing unnecessary paperwork when a petition is submitted, they should not be considered an acceptable substitute for precise and clear petition requirements. The requirements should include the policy reasons behind them, and all interested parties should be informed equally about the requirements without needing to have permanent representatives in Washington.

A new applicant to the SEC or the FDA, an applicant who is an "outsider," has to hire someone with personal knowledge of the "regulatory process" since each agency operates more like a country club than a democratic public agency. That statement is not made to question the integrity of the officials of those agencies but to point out that knowledge of the procedures is not as open, articulated, and predictable as it should be for the operation of an efficient agency of the federal government. Agencies like the SEC, the FCC, and the FDA are the reason why Washington law firms hire former government employees whose jobs are predicated on "knowing the federal system."

Intensity of Review

Once Congress has determined what needs to be regulated, who needs to be regulated, and by what standards or methods regulation is to be carried out, consideration must be given to the practical question of what degree of review is necessary to carry out the regulation activity. As mentioned, there are two basic approaches to an agency's review of cases, comprehensive and selective oversight. The intensity of agency review has a significant impact on the paperwork/information costs as it is far less costly to review only a portion of all possible cases—to employ the selective oversight approach.

As discussed in the preceding section on standards development, selective coverage of applications by the FCC and the FDA is not an appropriate management practice when weighed against the potential harm to the public. Consequently the petition process for both agencies is relatively costly and time consuming. For example, the total time required to secure approval for an FM station is three to four months and fourteen months for an AM station; the minimum cost to an applicant is $4,000–$5,000, and the cost can run into millions of dollars if extensive hearings are required. Approval of an FDA petition can take up to two years and cost the applicant a minimum of $400,000 for the necessary chemical and toxicological studies.

The SEC, however, has instituted a unique system of tiered levels of review, which provides a practical administrative tool for performing the approval function expeditiously and more nearly within the twenty-day statutory period. After a preliminary check by the Office of Registration and Information Service at the SEC, a registration statement is assigned, through a random process, to one of the fifteen branch chiefs in the Division of Corporate Finance. The branch chief screens the registration statement and determines the category of review: (1) customary, (2) cursory, (3) summary, or (4) deferred. A brief description of each type of review follows:

1. *Customary.* Formal criteria for full disclosure are contained in the Securities Act of 1933 as well as the SEC rules and regulations. Customary review is designed to ensure full disclosure. Each filing is reviewed by an examiner—either an attorney or a financial analyst—as well as an accountant. The accountant checks the adequacy of the financial statement, and the examiner deals primarily with the text of the prospectus.
2. *Cursory.* The registration statement is declared effective without detailed review or written or oral comments. Letters

are required from the chief executive of the corporation, accountants, and managing underwriters on behalf of all the underwriters stating that they are aware that the review is only cursory and that they are aware of their statutory responsibilities.

3. *Summary.* A limited review is made, and a small amount of additional information is requested. Once the additional information is received and commented upon, the registration statement is declared effective but the same assurances required for cursory review must be made.

4. *Deferred.* The registration statement is so poorly prepared or patently defective that it is rejected without staff review or comment. The applicant can either withdraw the statement or amend it.

The type of review conducted and its extensiveness depends in part on the type of offering. Stock offerings can be of three broad types: (1) new offerings from a new company (about sixty per year), (2) new offerings from a company already registered with the SEC (about twenty-three hundred per year), and (3) modifications and/or updates of existing offerings. Within the category of new offerings by registered companies, a further subdivision is made to differentiate between companies that frequently issue new stock and those that do so only occasionally. This distinction is important since much of the information used to determine adequate disclosure is general information about the company, its financial conditions, and its activities.

A second key criterion for determining the degree of review is the type of offering being made. In recent years, the SEC has adopted certain short forms, notably Forms S-7 and S-16, that do not require disclosure of matters already covered in reports and proxy material filed or distributed under provisions of the Securities Exchange Act. Another short form for registration under the Securities Exchange Act is Form S-8 for the registration of securities to be offered only to employees of the issuing company and its subsidiaries. The commission has proposed amendments to Form S-8 that are designed to reduce the issuers' cost and burden of registration and still be consistent with the objective of protecting investors by increasing the availability of the form to more types of employee plans, particularly certain option plans that may not receive special tax treatment under the Internal Revenue Code.

Because current information on corporations is required and maintained by the SEC or the securities exchanges, the varied levels of review are practical. This situation does not exist for the FCC or the FDA. Needed information is not already available, nor would the costs of obtaining and maintaining such information appear to outweigh the value of having it on hand.

Monitoring and Enforcement

All three agencies use a combination of preventative monitoring techniques and punitive enforcement techniques such as fines and criminal prosecution. Rather surprisingly, all three agencies rely primarily on complaints from citizens for monitoring rather than relying to any great extent on reports and record keeping. In the area of enforcement, however, each of the agencies relies on a different method. The FCC relies heavily on fines; the SEC, on court injunctions; and the FDA, on manufacturer recall. These differences are quite obviously the result of the different types of substantive area being regulated.

From an information/paperwork point of view, it is important to determine whether monitoring and enforcement are decentralized or centralized, i.e., are they conducted primarily in the field or from Washington? If carried out in the field, are they directly supervised and controlled by Washington or does Washington merely provide selective overview? Presumably, the regulatory process is less paperwork intensive and time consuming if the operation is centralized and more costly if decentralized with constant supervision by Washington.

The SEC and the FDA use field offices, with oversight by Washington, to carry out monitoring activities. The FCC has both a decentralized technical inspection staff composed of engineers and operated by the field offices and a centralized internal-station-operation inspection staff composed of attorneys under the direct supervision of the Washington office. The dual system seems redundant. Persons trained in both areas are no doubt available and would eliminate the necessity for dual offices and dual inspections and monitoring. If a sufficient number of personnel knowledgeable in both areas is lacking, using a team that consists of an engineer and an attorney and is directed by one office would seem more efficient and less paperwork intensive.

From an overall standpoint, the FDA has the most effective enforcement procedure with the least attendant cost and man-hour burden. For the most part, its regulatory strategy is anticipatory rather than reactive, preventive rather than corrective. Although the agency has precise guidelines for recalling products, it tries to ensure that safety is built into the products it regulates. It relies on the voluntary efforts of the industry to regulate itself and to pay for all such costs, with the threat of seizure for noncompliance. Ensuring that the burden remains on the industry itself is an effective method that other agencies might pursue more vigorously. Although the SEC starts out with such an assumption, it is abandoned by the time it comes to enforcement. Consequently an inordinate amount of staff time is expended in enforcement activities.

One novel administrative practice employed by the SEC as a preventative measure rather than as a corrective method of enforcement is the "no action letter." To help the regulated companies prevent a questionable matter from developing into a problem, these letters allow a company to ask the SEC for approval of a proposal, which assures the company that its proposal is valid.

In general, each agency permits broad staff discretion in enforcement activities and appears sensitive to the need for penalties that are consistent with the gravity of the violation. Although an effective method of enforcement might be to impose large fines or severe criminal penalties on a few violators as an example to other potential violators, such a technique is spurned by the three agencies. Perhaps publicizing a few cases of flagrant violations that are penalized vigorously and sternly should be considered, since all three agencies conduct their investigations as informally as possible and with as little public notice as possible. Simple publicity might be an effective and inexpensive deterrent.

THE ICC, THE CAB, THE FMC, AND THE FCC

This study examines four federal agencies that regulate, in the public interest, various aspects of interstate and U.S.-foreign transportation and shipping. They are (1) the Interstate Commerce

Commission, responsible for the regulation of interstate surface transportation; (2) the Civil Aeronautics Board, responsible for the regulation of the civil air-transport industry; (3) the Federal Maritime Commission, responsible for the regulation of waterborne foreign and domestic offshore commerce; and (4) the Federal Communications Commission, responsible for the regulation of interstate and U.S.-foreign communications by radio, television, wire, and cable. (Because the FCC approves rates for common carriers, it was included in this comparative study as well as in the previous one.)

The major forms of regulation are the approval of proposed common-carrier rates, approval of proposed agreements and corporate relationships, and the licensing or certification of all groups of carriers that provide transportation service. The agencies also engage in activities such as enforcement and monitoring to increase their regulatory effectiveness.

The specific areas of comparison among these three agencies are the administrative practices related to the approval of common-carrier rates and the supporting activities of monitoring and enforcement. To provide a frame of reference, Table 7.1 presents informa-

Table 7.1

Comparison of Regulatory Activities

	ICC	CAB	FMC	FCC[1]
Estimated total number of regulated units	19,044	400	211	1,621
Estimated number of major units	2,000	10	15	11
Total budget	$49,970,000	$17,610,000	$7,300,000	$50,512,662
Estimated total staff	2,098	717	310	1,835

tion on the total number of regulated units, the number of major units (which together constitute 80 percent of the market), and the overall budget and staff figures for each agency.

Rate Approval Process

There are many ways to determine shipping and transportation rates. The two most basic are the setting of rates through the free market and government regulation of rates.[11] Within the latter category there are again two methods of rate setting: an agency sets the rates rather than industry and an agency reviews rates set by industry. The review method comprises two alternative approaches to rate regulation, both of which have merit and disadvantages. One approach is to design and enforce agency-developed "rate standards" that specify exactly what types of rate changes are justified and on what basis. Another approach is to review all proposed rates.

The four regulatory agencies examined in this section all employ the rate review process as a method of rate regulation, which provides a foundation for the comparison of their regulatory rate-making practices. In keeping with the previously outlined comparative study format, the administrative practices used to regulate rates of the ICC, the FMC, the CAB, and the FCC are contrasted in terms of the following activities: rules development, rules implementation, and monitoring and enforcement.

Rules Development

Specificity of Legislation and Clarity of Administrative Rules

As mentioned earlier, the development of rules and standards constitutes the initial activity of any regulatory process and involves specificity of legislation, clarity of administrative rules, and the coverage of rules.

The degree of specificity of legislation and the clarity of administrative rules vary greatly among federal agencies, and we suggest that this degree or range of variance has significant implications in terms of paperwork activities. There is little difference between ICC, CAB, and FMC legislation with regard to rate making. CAB legislation and ICC legislation state generally that rates should not be unjust or unreasonable, unjustly discriminatory, or unduly prejudicial or preferential, and FMC legislation stipulates that rates should not be too high or too low or detrimental to U.S. commerce. Similarly a comparison of the administrative interpretations of the legislation by the agencies yields only a slight contrast. All have a history that is characterized by varied interpretations and numerous legislative appeals.

The administrative rules of the agencies also illustrate varying degrees of clarity.[12] At one extreme is the CAB, which has recently adopted an overall 12-percent rate of return on investment;[13] at the other extreme is the FMC, in which decisions are based on negotiations between shippers and carriers. ICC standards also lack clarity and rigor, and that agency's rate decisions are based primarily on precedent and judgment. The vagueness of the legislative mandates for these agencies often has resulted in decisions based on negotiation and precedent. It might be argued that negotiation and precedent may provide, albeit informally, a certain amount of rigor and clarity because they may result in a relatively consistent pattern of rate approval that the carriers no doubt follow closely and understand reasonably well. However, our conclusion is that sooner or later decisions based on negotiation and precedent lead to ambiguity and/or the exercise of discretion on the part of the decision makers. Both results are paperwork/information intensive. Furthermore, imprecise rules encourage carriers to attempt to push through many rate proposals that they would not propose were there more precisely defined rate rules.

Coverage of Rules and Caseload Burden

It has already been mentioned that there are two basic approaches toward the coverage of regulatory rules, comprehensive and selective oversight, and that if based on the greatest problem areas, selective coverage is in most cases a more cost-effective method of regulation than is comprehensive coverage. From a management point of view, comprehensive coverage (i.e., coverage of the smallest problems as well as the largest ones) is necessary only when minor violations can result in a serious problem such as death. All of the agencies regulating transportation and shipping employ a type of comprehensive coverage, examining every application for a rate change for compliance with procedural regulations. This "procedural

Table 7.2

Caseload Burden for Selected Regulatory Agencies

Agency	No. of Cases Annually	No. of Staff to Review Cases	Caseload to Staff Ratio
FMC	12,000 Domestic Tariff Pages	23	522
CAB	147,000 Tariff Pages	32	4,594
ICC	600,000 Tariff Pages	135	4,444

Source: Data compiled by the Federal Paperwork Commission.

review" checks tariff applications for such things as the inclusion of specific data and the proper format. However, none of the agencies conducts a thorough, substantive review of all rates, i.e., a review that examines whether a rate is economically justified and fair and reasonable.

Table 7.2 presents agency caseload burdens in terms of the number of rate proposals requiring review and the number of staff to carry out the review. The figures indicate that all three agencies have large caseload burdens, making a thorough review of all rate cases virtually impossible. Thus, the agencies have developed several approaches to minimize the number of thorough rate reviews performed. The FCC explores substantive issues during the procedural comprehensive review, but it will perform an extensive substantive review only on rate proposals that raise particularly significant questions. Another variation is the FMC approach, which involves thorough substantive reviews of all general rate increases and decreases. However, in terms of specific rate changes, the agency reviews extensively only those requests that appear particularly questionable or that entail the setting of new precedents. The ICC and the CAB review only those rates that raised questions during the procedural review or that prompted a complaint by another carrier or shipper.

These practices suggest that although manpower and resource constraints should not be the only determinants of the extensiveness of review coverage, those factors greatly influence the thoroughness of agency reviews. Given limited resources, agencies faced with an excessive number of cases requiring review are virtually forced to develop some type of case-screening techniques to determine the proper degree of review intensity required for each case. Thus, heavy caseload burdens prompt agencies to explore approaches that reduce the paperwork intensity of the review activity.

Implementation of Rules

The implementation of rate standards or rules occurs during the rate approval process, which reviews and then rejects or approves proposed rates. The idea behind this process is that an agency acts as an overseer, not a setter, of rates set by industry. The system generally operates in the following manner. A cursory overview is given to all proposed tariffs to check for compliance with procedural rules. This overview provides the agency with enough information to make a rate approval decision in most cases. The small number of tariffs that raise questions during this procedural review are reviewed further and more substantively. If, after the substantive review, questions concerning the lawfulness of the proposed rate still exist (in terms of its economic effects on the market, consumers, and shippers) or if a shipper or another carrier protests the proposed rate by submitting a petition, the commissioners or board members review the case and may order a suspension or an investigation of the proposed rate. A hearing before an administrative law judge is then conducted. The judge makes an initial decision and, depending on the agency and the circumstances, the commissioners or board members then make a final decision. At different points throughout the process, there is an opportunity for the carriers to appeal the orders and decisions. Final recourse for the carriers who wish to appeal an agency's decision is to the federal courts.

Data Required in Support of Proposed Rate

There are differences in the rate approval process among the agencies. One variation concerns the amount of financial and economic data required for a rate change proposal. Conceivably such information could be required later in the process and only in the event that a rate change prompts serious questions. The CAB and the FCC require that economic data, which vary according to the type of rate, accompany all proposed tariffs. The ICC and the FMC require that specific economic data be submitted for all general rate changes (and for proposed new routes of vessel operators at the FMC), but they make data requirements optional for all specific increases.

Insofar as many proposed rate changes do not get reviewed thoroughly, the method employed by the FMC and the ICC, which requires that supportive economic and financial data accompany only those proposed rates that do undergo extensive review, seems to be reasonable and to involve minimal paperwork activity.

Staff Background

Presumably the kind of staff responsible for reviewing tariffs influences the kind of considerations that are made during the review and thus the type of decisions that result. The task of reviewing proposed rates involves a number of skills and disciplines including industrial specialists, lawyers, economists, and accountants—all of which are represented, in varying degrees, at the agencies. For example, all four agencies employ industrial specialists to review the proposed rates for procedural compliance. But the composition of the staffs responsible for conducting substantive rate reviews varies among the agencies. Table 7.3 indicates the professional back-

Table 7.3

Backgrounds and Agency Decision Criteria

Agency	Type of Professional Staff	Type of Decision Criteria for Rate Reviews
ICC	Attorneys	Precedent and Judgment
CAB	Economists	Precise Economic Criteria
FMC	Economists and Accountants	Negotiation and Precedent
FCC	Attorneys and Accountants	Precise Economic Criteria

grounds of the substantive review staffs and the type of decision criteria employed by each agency for rate reviews.

Although the table suggests that there is a correlation between the professional background of a staff and the type of criteria it uses to make rate approval decisions, it must be noted that these review staffs have varying degrees of influence on the rate decisions. Thus, in an agency that does not give much decision authority to the substantive review staff, the criteria for the final decision may not reflect the professional background of the review staff. This is the case in the FMC where, despite financial and economic reviews, rate decisions are ultimately based on negotiations and precedent.

The background of the review staff affects the amount of paperwork generated by the review process. A background that predisposes the reviewers to think in terms of precise decision criteria promotes less paperwork/information activity than a background that predisposes the reviewers to regard each case as unique and therefore subject to broad discretion.

Type and Location of Decision Authority Units and Opportunities for Carrier Appeal

The regulatory process includes many important and complex considerations. One such consideration involves the trade-off between ensuring that the regulatory process is relatively efficient, on the one hand, and allowing for due process, on the other hand. Quite clearly, there are costs and benefits associated with each objective. The idea, then, is to maximize the benefits and minimize the costs associated with both.

In terms of the rate approval process, an opportunity for carriers to appeal exists to ensure due process. However, the opportunity can result in lengthy procedures and time delays. Thus, it is of the utmost importance that the opportunities for appeal be reasonable both in terms of number and in terms of location. One important consideration in determining whether or not an appeal opportunity is both reasonable and necessary for ensuring due process is whether the decision that is to be appealed is, in fact, a decision that carries authority or a decision that is in reality only a recommendation.

The type and location of the organizational unit responsible for making rate decisions vary among agencies as do the type of opportunity for carrier appeal and unit to which the appeal may be presented. Table 7.4 presents information on the types of decision-making units, on the types of decisions that may be appealed, and on the types of units to which an appeal can be made.

With regard to regulatory efficiency and due process, Table 7.4 illustrates two important points: there is inconsistency and inefficiency in both. The ICC is an example of the former. Railroads are allowed three opportunities for appeal; motor carriers are allowed four. If three appeal opportunities ensure due process for railroads, there appears to be little evidence to support the need for four in the case of motor carriers. The FMC demonstrates the second point. The second decision that is allowed to be appealed is that of the administrative law judge, who does not wield true decision-making authority. The judge can make only a recommendation to the commissioners about what rate action should be taken; the commissioners then make the decision. Since the judge's decision carries no legal authority, it seems unnecessary to allow this decision to be appealed. The paperwork implications of these two superfluous steps are obvious: they are high in paperwork burden and low in paperwork value.

Existence of a Refund Clause

Another variation among agencies with regard to the petition process concerns a refund clause, which authorizes an agency to award retroactive payments to shippers who have paid carriers a rate that went into effect but was eventually determined to be illegal or unjustified. Such an issue arises because rates are allowed to become effective before a final decision on their legality is made, but the existence of a refund clause tends to deter carriers from attempting to push through an inordinate increase.

Each of the agencies has a different type of refund clause, or no refund clause at all. At one extreme is the ICC, which, in the case of motor carriers, has the discretion to require a "keep account order" (an order requiring a carrier to maintain accounts of the moneys accrued because of a rate increase) for investigation cases and for those investigation and suspension cases in which the suspension period terminates before the case is decided. The records kept because of a keep account order can then be used as the basis for making refunds to shippers if an effective rate is judged unlawful. In the case of the railroads, new legislation (the 4-R Act) has altered

Table 7.4

Appeal Structure

Agency	Decision-making Units	Decision Allowed to be Appealed	Unit to Which Appeal is Made
ICC	Substantive Review staff	Order to suspend and/or investigate	Division Two[1]
	Administrative law judge (ALJ)	ALJ decision	Review Board
	Review Board	Review Board Decision	Division Two
	Division Two[2]	Division Two decision	Division Two
	Division Two[3]	Division Two decision	Full Commission
CAB	Commissioners	Order to suspend and/or investigate	Commissioners
	Administrative law judge	ALJ decision	Commissioners
	Commissioners	Commissioners' decision	Commissioners
FMC	Commissioners	Order to suspend and/or investigate	Commissioners
	Commissioners	ALJ decision	Commissioners
	Commissioners	Commissioners' decision	Commissioners

[1]Most often, the highest level of decision-making authority for rate cases in the ICC is Division Two (composed of three commissioners).

[2]The new rail legislation omits this step; i.e., railroads can only make one further appeal after the appeal of an ALJ decision, with the exception of a "General Transportation of Importance."

[3]This opportunity for both motor and rail carrier appeal is called a "General Transportation of Importance." It is rarely used, and can only be made if there is clear and convincing new evidence or changed circumstances.

the system. Although its precise intent is rather unclear, the legislation limits the length of an investigation and suspension proceeding to the length of the suspension period. Thus, except for investigation cases in which the refund clause operates as it does for motor carriers, the refund clause is unnecessary because a final decision must be made before the suspension period terminates. The FMC has no refund clause at all even though increased rates may be charged before they receive final approval. The FCC has a refund clause, but it stipulates that the refund authority may be used only if the agency can prove that a questionable rate is unlawful and that there is a reasonable, existing rate for another carrier whose circumstances are identical to those of the carrier in question. This latter requirement is difficult to prove, which tends to limit the use of the refund clause. At the CAB, a new rate does not become effective until its legality is determined. There is, therefore, no need for a refund clause.

Clearly it is not desirable to create incentives for carriers to drag out the rate approval process, thereby exhausting time and resources and producing more paperwork. But the lack of a refund clause can do just that by not "punishing" carriers for rate proposals that are eventually judged to be unlawful.

Public Concern

Although it would seem appropriate for the public to be involved in the development of administrative rules, the study found that most involvement occurs later, during the rate approval process. Even then, citizens, or rather the consumers, are not politically and economically organized enough to represent themselves before the commissioners, so the agencies make various attempts to represent the consumers' viewpoint during the rate approval process. The ICC, the CAB, and the FMC all have some type of consumer unit concerned with rate matters. Specifically, the CAB has a consumer advocate's office that acts as an independent party and represents the consumer when rates are set and in rate case proceedings. The ICC has a consumer unit in the tariff section, and it examines the impact of proposed rates on consumers and makes recommendations to the ICC for rate suspensions or investigations. The FMC has just created a consumer unit, but its mandate is uncertain at this time.

Bringing the consumer into the rate approval process has both high paperwork/information costs and many benefits. It can be done in several ways, one approach being to allocate agency funds to pay a consumer representative to present consumer petitions during rate case proceedings. A second approach is to create an agency unit to analyze rate proposals from the consumer's perspective. The latter approach would seem to be the most cost-effective method, insofar as an agency's staff is made up of experienced professionals who are well acquainted with the subject.

Monitoring and Enforcement

The agencies have various approaches to the enforcement of agency regulations: some rely on preventative measures or on monitoring techniques such as reporting and record-keeping requirements, audits, and investigations; others use punitive measures such as the levying of heavy fines. Furthermore, in dealing with violations, some agencies rely on administrative procedures and penalties, and others favor federal court procedures and penalties.

In terms of the general approach to enforcement of agency programs and regulations, the ICC, the CAB, and the FMC show little variance. All three agencies emphasize monitoring techniques, which require reporting and recordkeeping of carrier operations from both an economic and a financial perspective. In 1976, it took the FMC 4.5 man-years to process such reports; it took the ICC 2–4 man-years. Similarly, all three agencies audit carrier financial records. In 1976, the ICC conducted 1,455 audits on carrier financial accounts, which took 58 man-years, and 16,738 audits called compliance surveys, which took 63 man-years. Only 4 financial audits were conducted by the FMC in the same year. A significant number of field investigations are also conducted by all three agencies. In 1976, the ICC conducted 1,024 such investigations representing roughly 56 man-years, the CAB devoted 16 man-years to field investigations, and the FMC spent 36 man-years on 625 field investigations.

All three agencies rely extensively on punitive measures. In 1976, $1,735,183 were collected from 577 carriers involved in cases concerning ICC regulations, over $1,480,125 were collected from 55 carriers involved in CAB cases, and roughly $356,707 were paid out by 34 carriers involved in FMC-related cases. All together, these measures represented fewer than 10 man-years.

Agency reliance on administrative enforcement procedures versus federal court procedures varies somewhat. At the ICC during 1976, there were 42 cease-and-desist orders, 104 commission proceedings, and 353 civil forfeitures as opposed to 94 civil injunctions and 74 criminal cases. Of the $1,735,183 in fines collected from carriers in ICC-related cases, only $206,450 were levied by the courts. These figures suggest that the ICC has a preference for exhausting its administrative procedures before involving the federal courts. During the same year, the FMC had 31 civil forfeiture cases and only 3 cases were referred to the Department of Justice. Those 3 cases, however, resulted in more than half the total of carrier fines in 1976. Similarly, in 1976 the CAB issued or sought the issuance of 51 cease-and-desist orders. Only 36 cases were referred to the federal courts, including 7 civil injunctions and 10 criminal proceedings. A change of CAB enforcement bureau directors has resulted in a shift to a reliance on court injunctions rather than cease-and-desist orders, and fines levied by the federal courts have come to represent more than half the total of carrier fines in CAB-related cases.

From a paperwork/information standpoint, low monitoring accompanied by harsh penalties seems to be a more cost-effective method of enforcement than high monitoring and low penalties. As described above, the ICC, the CAB, and the FMC approaches to enforcement combine elements of both methods. That is, they all rely on monitoring techniques and punitive measures in their enforcement activities although neither is relied upon predominantly. It should be noted, however, that the enforcement strategy of low monitoring and high penalties can also be paperwork intensive. As is the case in the above three agencies, this is true when penalties in the form of fines are levied by the federal courts and thus are a part of extensive court paperwork and procedures.

8
Management Information Systems

Introduction

A management information system (MIS) can be defined as "the structure and process through which an organization identifies, obtains, evaluates, transfers, and utilizes information, both internally and externally, so that the organization may operate and advance toward fulfilling its objective." It is a system that provides management with the information it requires to make decisions, evaluate alternatives, monitor progress, measure performance, and detect situations requiring corrective action.[1] Any organization has an information flow that serves, in varying degrees, all the component parts (divisions, departments, etc.) and members of the organization. When we speak of a MIS we are simply directing attention to that portion of the information system in which there is interaction with management.

A MIS entails hardware, software, people, and procedures; it can rely heavily on a data base management system (DBMS) or on key personnel; it may be a manual, a computer-based, or (in more appropriate terminology for today's system) a computer-communication-based information management system. Although the total cost of government MIS practices is unknown, the hardware and processing costs can be identified. The present expenditures for information processing in the executive branch are estimated to be around $20 billion per year. The federal government has approximately 9,260 computers, of which 6,000 have been acquired in the last ten years. Expenditures for the automation of agency information systems were approximately $3.2 billion in 1975.

In discussing a MIS, one needs to emphasize that one is talking about a system of management. Management systems have two important characteristics that are relevant to any formal MIS. First, management systems are not static but are dynamic and, as such, require interaction among individuals. Good managers serve as intermediaries between various members of an organization and know how to ask the right questions in order to link the right people and resources together to produce effective results. Second, management systems are not necessarily rational in the scientific sense. For the most part, decision making cannot be traced from a Stage X "idea" (input) to a Stage Y "implementation" (output).

Unfortunately the exact opposite presumptions have characterized the MIS field to date. First, MIS is or has become equated and confused with electronic data processing (EDP) or automated data processing (ADP). When the "systems man" emerged as the central figure in the information field, it was believed that all information systems expertise and EDP and ADP specialists should be removed from the various functional departments and consolidated into a central service organization. This belief resulted in one of the greatest setbacks to computer utilization and caused the classic gap between the information system and the user. Too often the success of a particular MIS has been determined by the magnitude of the computer memory bank. The premise has been, "We have this computer technology available; how can we apply it to the information needs of particular clients?" Instead, the premise should be, "We have these problems; what techniques can we apply to help solve them?"

Second, the planners and users of MIS have approached problem solving as a totally rational and logical thinking process; the opportunity for creative thinking has been obstructed and decision makers have been made into processors of information. Those who support MIS have refused to accept the facts that some problems are solved simply by chance and that no matter how integrated the data base of a system there will always remain data sources that cannot be integrated whether for technical, political, or administrative reasons. In short, MIS is a closed-end process that has headed us in the wrong direction.

The following sections discuss the more common problems associated with MIS and outline the direction MIS should take in order to be a valuable information tool and an effective method for managing information.

Customizing Systems to User Needs

Two primary tasks of MIS are to provide information of value to decision makers and to reduce paperwork/information burdens. Federal MIS systems have failed to do either one effectively, mainly because MIS technicians and managers have refused to customize the system to the needs of federal decision makers. All too often the information specialist is really an EDP specialist—a computer technician. These technicians and managers have directed their energies toward quantity of data rather than value of information; they have emphasized system construction, not system analysis and evaluation. As a result, the systems are useless to most decision makers.

A good case in point is the Office of Economic Opportunity (OEO). That agency was instructed to collect information on all federal government expenditures and to break it down by areas. An expensive computer system was developed and maintained for this effort, but statistics indicate it was infrequently used. In another case, a top-level policymaker in the OEO decided the agency should have a computer capability to break down socio-economic characteristics and OEO activities by congressional districts. An outside firm was hired to develop the data base and programming materials. The firm provided what was stipulated under contract, but it neglected to provide the OEO with the documentation needed to update the system. The result was that after spending more than one million dollars on initial start-up, the system was inoperative within a year. Many other federal agencies have systems, developed from scratch at considerable expense to the American taxpayer, that are equally ineffective.

Federal information managers tend to use obsolete systems rather than to confront the information technician in order to update a system. Decision makers, therefore, are forced to concentrate on other methods of securing necessary information, and, as a consequence, information activities have increased rather than decreased.

In order to provide information of value with the least amount of burden, a MIS should be designed to suit management functions and be directed toward specific user needs. In short, it must be a tool for problem solving. A good information manager should ask and seek answers to the following types of questions.

1. What is the context for a decision? What is the purpose of the particular program for which this system is being designed? Who is supposed to be served, i.e., who are the clients? What are the economic, political, social, and psychological constraints operating upon this organization that will influence and affect any decision?

2. What are the needs? Whose needs are being fed into this proposed system? Can they be routinized? What proportion of the overall needs can be covered by a routinized system? Where do the various needs of the organization's subunits conflict with each other?

3. What is the appropriate formating/packaging? How many people will be receiving this information? What are their educational and professional backgrounds? What format are they familiar with? What format or media are people most comfortable with?

Having delimited the policy context, the constraints, the needs, and the format, the information manager must then determine the means by which information of value can be provided. He should ask such questions as, Can this be done through computer technology? Is it necessary to have an intermediary? If so, should the intermediary be asking himself, Do I fully understand the problems being faced? Do I understand what information the clients have at hand and what information can be obtained through other sources? What other resources can be brought to bear on the problem if the system is not obtaining the relevant information? Can this be done within the time constraints set for this problem? After asking such questions and determining their answers, the information manager is then ready to design and implement the appropriate information system. Once the information is provided, the information manager should then determine how much it helps in solving the problem. This determination will provide the necessary feedback so the MIS is not a closed, static system but an open, dynamic system geared to user needs.

Accuracy and Complexity

Frequently management information systems can be criticized for complexity and/or inaccuracy. In concentrating on the production of information instead of problem solving, MIS has added to infor-

mation complexity and overload. Sophisticated and expensive systems have been built that far exceed the grasp of potential users,
and, as a result, many expensive management systems are simply
not used.

Again, the OEO is a good case in point. That agency decided it
should have a computerized system to monitor the development of
community action programs through data supplied by community
action field personnel. But the field personnel refused to cooperate,
the data were consequently inaccurate, and the information was not
used. Nevertheless, the data continued to be collected, processed,
and printed for several years, and large piles of unused printouts
were a common sight in OEO offices.

Another example illustrating the problem of obtaining accurate information is the Vietnam Hamlet Evaluation System. Soon after the
United States became engaged in war in Vietnam, Secretary of
Defense Robert McNamara asked his staff to develop an information system that would provide quantitative information on changes
in political and military circumstances throughout Vietnam. In
response, an extremely complex and expensive computerized system
was developed, and it was impressive conceptually and operationally. A large amount of data was collected on each hamlet in South
Vietnam; these data were then converted into indexes of military
security, political security, and determinants thereof. The indexes
were subject to regular updates and special updates when circumstances changed dramatically. All the data were fed into a computer, making it possible for the Department of Defense and the
White House to obtain a current visual or quantitative picture of
the situation in one hamlet or in any aggregate grouping of hamlets.

Unfortunately the system failed to meet federal user needs, and
even more unfortunately, it contributed to some serious military
miscalculations. Primarily it failed because inaccurate data were received from the field. Not realizing that the data submitted were going to play a critical role in developing military strategies, the field
data collectors placed priority on other responsibilities that they
believed were more important. Furthermore, updating the data was
extremely time consuming and was rarely done. But more importantly, field personnel were required to make a number of qualitative judgments, and there was no way to ensure that those judgments were made in a standardized, comparable manner. Field

collectors sensed that their performance was being judged by the data submitted; i.e., they assumed that the more politically and militarily secure their hamlets appeared, the better their performance rating would be. This misunderstanding resulted in the data being overly optimistic, and, as a direct consequence, the military continually underestimated the resources needed to attain military objectives. Field personnel also mistook indicators for desired objectives. For example, the number of police in a hamlet was used as an indicator of hamlet security. But thinking that a larger number was desirable, the field personnel would enlist hamlet dwellers as policemen. Since the hamlet dwellers lacked training and equipment, they should not have been valued as highly as regular Vietnamese police.

Several important messages are to be gleaned from these examples. An information system is only useful if it contains information of value; inaccurate information in a MIS has no value. At the same time, inaccurate information is sometimes used which results in bad policy decisions that are often injurious to the public. If, on the other hand, inaccurate information is not used, that fact does not reduce the overall information burdens. In fact, it contributes to their acceleration as a decision maker will turn to other sources for the requisite information.

Problem of Privacy

Information is power. The existing pattern of information flow and usage is a vital part of the power structure of an organization. New systems, new disciplines, and new information flows all serve to disrupt the pattern. The information specialist, as an agent of change, is obviously in the middle and in one of the most political jobs of a company or an agency. Most information specialists realize this, but most fail dismally in trying to learn how to deal with the situation.

It is essential that the political dynamics associated with the linkage between information access and control and management control be recognized. An information system is designed and built in a political environment, in a climate of user suspicion and management anxiety and of considerable uncertainty concerning the cost, schedule, and value of the system. The system becomes an agent of change that will be welcomed by some and resisted vehemently by others. A completely new form of discipline must be imposed on all components and members of an organization. Certain "freedoms" that were tolerated by a loosely structured, personal kind of management system are lost. Thus, personal contact may be regimented, uniformity may be substituted for diversity, automated, electronic funds transfer may eliminate consumer float, and the ability to obtain useful management information may be constrained by the new system. Human will and people-to-people dealings are potentially subordinate to the will of the information machine. One of the greatest tasks of information management and general management is to prevent this subordination from occurring. It will become a vital task when national information systems are designed and sufficient safeguards must be provided to prevent a total dehumanization and lack of personal privacy.

It is important to recognize that the processing and handling of information are not as equally distributed as the accessibility and intelligibility of information in our society. Thus, information power and, in turn, control are likewise distributed unequally. This established a political arena for information policies and practices of the government (and other institutions) as well as a pattern of use that governs access, dissemination, and appropriateness. At present, this pattern of use has low public visibility because of a general lack of understanding about the role of information and the relationship between information and power. There is also ignorance of the concept of an information society and its implications. This lack of understanding is unfortunate as it augments the manipulatory potential of those in control and also permits them to thwart new information systems that can alter the existing pattern of use and control.

Conclusions and Recommendations

Management information systems originated and matured around new, automated information-handling technologies, most noticeably the computer. The need for an intermediary to make the computer useful created a dependency on the "systems person" or EDP professional. These "information" specialists have confused data with information and data management systems with management information systems. Thus, there is too much emphasis on hardware, and insufficient attention is given to the initial definition and description of information needs, the determination of information value, and those features that can make an information system useful. We are still using a cost-benefit calculus that best fits the evaluation of clerical cost reductions that result from implementing a simple data-processing task.

With advances in technology and incremental integration, system evaluation and justification have become complex, yet we fail to develop rigorous criteria. Many costs and benefits are indivisible and intangible or incommensurable. Many are hidden, subtle, or "externalized" so that we fail to account for or rationalize their neglect. It is human to focus on the calculable rather than to wrestle with the incalculable. We tend to build systems before having an adequate and a competent conception and evaluation of what its usefulness will be, often ensuring their deficiency and failure. Sensing that we did not build the right system, we leap right back in and build anew rather than face up to the need for a painful reexamination and reevaluation of needs and value.

An effective MIS must help to specify "value." In this regard, it can play a vital role in assisting policymakers in the areas of problem identification, development of options, choosing among options, program design, program implementaton, program monitoring and evaluation, and program redesign and replication. To attain these ends, a MIS must be tailored to the needs of the potential users. The following steps are recommended.

1. Value/burden assessments of selected information from large-scale and smaller-sized information systems should be conducted.
2. Systems should be designed on the basis of the users' needs rather than systems technology.
3. Experience with successful systems should be transmitted to other agencies and programs contemplating the development or expansion of large-scale systems.
4. Differences in the technical capabilities of potential and actual providers of "data" to the systems should be identified and considered when decisions are made to collect the information or to compensate respondents for providing the information required.

5. The technical capabilities of and the equality of access for potential government and nongovernment users should be identified and considered when making decisions to collect information for the government.

With the introduction of these types of changes, we expect that management information systems would help to increase the value of information to its users.

Federal Evaluation Practices

Introduction

The federal government currently spends upward of $1 billion annually on formal evaluation activities. In addition to these formal evaluations, both the Office of Management and Budget and the Congress carry out informal evaluations during their respective budget-review, authorization, and appropriation activities. The basic justification given for performing evaluations is that they provide data on the basis of some objective criteria for use in making more rational decisions. In short, evaluations are thought to contribute to better decision making.

By using the definition of the "value of information" developed in Chapter 4, one can discern how closely the techniques of evaluation fit the needs of decision makers. Information has value if it

- contributes to implementing, operating, and monitoring federal programs that are responsive to citizens' needs;
- assists citizens and decision makers in understanding, evaluating, and implementing what the government is doing and knowing whether the government is acting appropriately and within its responsibilities;
- assists citizens to obtain government goods and services to which they are entitled; and
- makes an essential contribution to the operation of a federal program that is responsive to citizens' needs.

Evaluation methodology that centers on assessing the needs of citizens and the efficiency and effectiveness of programs designed to meet those needs can be a highly useful tool for decision makers and can provide the foundation for realizing the value of information.

One major use of evaluation information is to help in program assessment. Once national objectives and priorities are determined,
specific programs are established to meet those objectives. Evaluations can then be employed to assess those programs. The question
that evaluation information can help answer is, Does the program do
what it was expected to do when it was established and is it still relevant to the overall objectives of the nation? With Congress considering the enactment of "sunset" legislation, evaluation information is
a necessity in determining which programs will be renewed and
which ones will be allowed to expire. The second major use of
evaluation information is to provide data for planning. Evaluations
can provide vital information on the likely impact and probable consequences of a particular policy and thus enable a decision maker to
make meaningful comparisons and appropriate choices when allocating scarce resources.

Unfortunately, evaluation practices have fallen far short of meeting those needs and of realizing their full potential. Because evaluations have not been structured for federal policymakers, they have
not been seen by those decision makers as a form of policy analysis;
nor have evaluations been viewed by federal administrators as a
primary management and monitoring tool. Even worse, in some
cases evaluation information has been misused and has been the
source of injurious federal policy decisions.

The following discussion of the major problems of federal evaluation practices emphasizes that the value of these practices should be
increased and their burden should be reduced. The problem areas
are as follows:

1. How to Increase the Value of Federal Evaluations
   a. the link to national priorities and objectives
   b. increasing utilization
   c. technical problems related to evaluations
   d. political uses of evaluation
2. How to Decrease the Burden of Federal Evaluations
   a. reducing the communications gap
   b. congressional initiatives

For the purposes of this analysis, evaluation means (1) the systematic gathering and assessment of information to determine the need

for a social program/action or (2) an assessment of the impact of a program/action along with its possible costs and side effects. In the federal policymaking system, the intent of evaluation should be to supply useful, timely information to policymakers facing decisions on whether to initiate, modify, curtail, or terminate action programs that are intended to increase the general welfare of the citizenry.

How to Increase the Value of Federal Evaluations

The Link to National Priorities and Objectives

Evaluations must address the overall social impact of programs with regard to the attainment of national objectives. Fortunately there is a growing realization both inside and outside government that there is a difference between monitoring and evaluating. Although it is necessary for monitoring purposes to know whether a particular project was completed as planned or whether a program is being administered properly, such activity is only a part of what is needed to serve the total evaluation purpose, which is to assess how well a program meets its objective of maximizing citizen well-being. The facts that the Army Corps of Engineers completed a bridge properly, adhered to the budget, and finished on time do not mean the project was successful if the bridge is part of a footpath in a ghost town.

In recent years, funds appropriated for general evaluations have lagged behind those appropriated for evaluations of limited program concerns. More money is spent to determine compliance with program standards than to assess whether an agency program or project has been successsful in reaching a national objective. Time and money have been diverted from evaluating the achievement of stated objectives and funneled to assessing subsidiary agency activities instead. This imbalance between evaluation and regulation-related research is not consistent with a commitment to continuous problem solving. Regulation is designed to adjust behavior once a program has been started and to prevent infractions of the law. It is not an active, continuous monitoring technique with built-in feedback mechanisms designed to influence future planning, nor does it ascertain the effects that general purpose programs are having on specific social objectives as mandated by Congress and the executive branch.

Increasing Utilization

Evaluations are of little value if they are not used to make programs better, and there is considerable evidence to indicate that federal evaluations are often not used.[1] There are several important reasons for this lack of use.

Packaging. Utilization studies have documented that evaluations are frequently presented in a form that policymakers cannot use. Three common defects in form are prolixity, obsolescence, and extraterritoriality. A policymaker does not have time to read through lengthy reports, he can do little with data that are presented after the critical policy decisions have been made, and clearly he cannot change things that are beyond his authority and domain.

If evaluations are to be useful in increasing citizen well-being, they must be in a readable, manageable, timely, and relevant form. Those based on methodology and technology have a limited use and are subject to wide misuse. For example, an evaluation of an education program for minorities that measured the IQ of each student before the start of the program and then the grades each student received in an effort to determine the success of the program, actually measured the students and not the success of the program.

To prevent this from happening a contracting office responsible for funding an evaluation program should be made responsible for formulating strict guidelines for the presentation of research results before funding is authorized. These guidelines should specify the type of commentary desired in the final report—the relationship of the data and the interpretation to programmatic and national goals format (tables, pages, executive summary). Such guidelines would serve the needs of producers and users of evaluation research. A user would be forced to define for the producer the specific purpose and use of the evaluation; the producer would be forced to present the information in a form that the user could understand and utilize.

Coverage. In the past, evaluations have served largely as a final grading exercise and not as an aid to program planning on a continuous basis. At the very most, ex post facto evaluations can do little more than offer lessons for the future, and frequently they do not even do this.

With the current emphasis on grading, the program manager is the central subject of the evaluation instead of the program. Donald T. Campbell has pointed out that federal evaluations, in addition to being ex post facto, also become ad hominem.[2] Consequently the program manager views evaluation as a threat. If the evaluation comes out badly, he might lose his job. Also the evaluator is in the unfortunate position of having to find something wrong with the program he is assessing. One evaluator has commented that if an evaluator does not find one or more serious defects in the program he has been hired to evaluate, one or two questions will be raised, either implicitly or explicitly: (1) Has the evaluation been thorough? (2) If there was nothing wrong with the program, why was the evaluation commissioned in the first place?

The results of the situation described above are unproductive. A threatened manager attempts to defend his mode of operation. If he succeeds, he can continue to operate as he has in the past; if he fails, he will be fired and replaced. Moreover, since the evaluation is primarily a personal grading exercise, it offers little useful advice to a new replacement.

The primary emphasis of evaluation activity within the federal government should be changed from conducting ex post facto, summative grading exercises to conducting evaluations at various points throughout the lifetime of a project. Evaluations should offer diagnostic and prescriptive information that sets forth what can be done to eliminate or ameliorate problems before or as they occur, and measures success and/or failure.

Procurement. The problems of packaging and coverage are often the direct result of inappropriate procurement practices. Generally, evaluation contracts are awarded to universities and other nonprofit organizations, and they tend to be method oriented rather than policy oriented. Consequently the evaluation data are usually in a form that cannot be easily used in the decision-making process. This contributes to the gap between the users who are policy oriented and the researchers who are tied to methodology and technology.[3]

Technical Problems Related to Evaluations

From a methodological standpoint, the design of most evaluation programs follows the same basic research pattern.

1. Establish an ordered list of program goals and objectives
2. Give a definition of the problem, including an assessment of existing resources
3. Design appropriate evaluation methods as early in the process as possible
4. Implement program evaluation design
5. Interpret results at several points in time (formative evaluation) or at the completion of the program (summative evaluation)
6. Make appropriate changes as indicated by the evaluation results

Another common feature of program evaluation studies is the identification or development of measures of effectiveness (outcome), methods of data collection, and other individualized features of design. To be useful at the federal level, evaluation technology will have to advance to the point that standardized techniques can be applied to highly varied situations to permit a comparison and combining of results that will lead to national conclusions.

As already noted, the basic evaluation pattern is based on comparing the status of programmatic goals at the time an evaluation is conducted with the ideal set (or expected progress toward the goal). To accomplish this, legislation calling for evaluation should be made more specific, for example, by requiring federal offices of policy, planning, and evaluation to report in open hearings to Congress on the relationship between the evaluations and the national goals and priorities.

Political Uses of Evaluation

David Cohen has pointed out that "Decision-making, of course, is a euphemism for the allocation of resources—money, position, authority, etc. Thus, to the extent that information is an instrument, basis, or excuse for changing power relationships within or among institutions, evaluation is a political activity."[4] There is no question that evaluation can have tremendously important political and economic implications. However, it should also be recognized that there are more and less scientific ways to carry out and use evaluations. Since the ultimate cost of evaluations will be borne by the citizens, it is imperative that the primary purposes of evaluations—to objectively appraise the import of programs for citizen well-being and to make suggestions for improvement—be vigorously pursued.

Evaluations should be free of value judgments, in terms of directing the research toward the advocacy of a particular policy, and they should provide as accurate a mirror image of reality as possible. Decision makers can then use the results to help them make a decision. This approach is an affirmation of the value of evaluation research for the purpose of solving continuing problems. Under assessment procedures of this type, there is a shift from advocating a specific reform to pointing out the seriousness of a problem and hence to persistence should the first solution fail. As Campbell succinctly describes the process:

> There is a serious problem. We propose to initiate Policy A on an experimental basis. If after five years there has been no significant improvement, we will shift to Policy B. By making explicit that a given situation is only one of several that the administrator or party could in good conscience advocate, and by having ready a plausible alternative, the administrator can afford honest evaluations of outcomes. Negative results and failure of the first program does not jeopardize his job, for his job is to keep after the program until something is found that works.[5]

If this approach is taken, the dangers of politicizing evaluations is minimized.

How to Decrease the Burden of Federal Evaluations

Reducing the Communications Gap

In reviewing federal evaluation efforts, it is clear that much of the input data that is the foundation of evaluation research must of necessity come from local programs. The federal funding mechanism may mandate the collection of the information, but the actual data collection usually occurs at a lower level and frequently passes through several levels before final processing. Although potentially both the local program managers and the federal decision makers may use the evaluation information for the same purposes, there is a difference of emphasis. Although both are concerned with planning —in order to meet the needs of the citizenry fairly, efficiently, and effectively—the federal decision maker has to consider national priorities when setting goals whereas the local program manager simply compares differences among census tracts. A federal decision maker may be more concerned with summative evaluations in order to make discrete decisions, such as whether to renew a contract or whether a contractor has fulfilled a contract in a cost-effective manner. A local program manager is more interested in comparative assessments that may suggest program modifications to make use of the most effective and efficient methods for meeting the program goals. Put another way, the federal decision maker may use evaluation for monitoring how policy is being carried out, making discrete judgments, or reinforcing or checking on the "political climate." At the state level, decision makers may use the same or similar data for similar purposes, and the local program manager who supplies the data may use it to obtain new or continued funding.

Although this comparison suggests an overlap between the federal decision maker and the local planner/program director, there is little interaction between the two in practice. Federally required evaluations are complied with at the local level primarily to keep the funds flowing. This fact raises an important question as to the reliability of an evaluation. Also, information produced at the local level is sent to Washington, but evaluation results usually are received back at the local level too late to be of much use.

If effective program implementations are to occur at the local and state levels, and if evaluations are to provide decision makers with ongoing data to monitor progress, then effective feedback systems must be designed to serve state, local, and federal officials. To ensure that this occurs, contracting offices should stipulate, in the original contract, the number of reports that must be made to the state and local offices.

Congressional Initiatives

Congressional hearings are replete with examples of specific requests by individual congressmen and senators for specific types of evaluative information. Frequently the requests call for expensive data collection and processing efforts even though they concern relatively inconsequential program activities (although they may sound exciting).

Although the authority of Congress to ask the executive branch for information should not be abridged, Congress should be made aware of, and hence partially responsible for, the costs of its information requests. For example, when Congress requests information from federal agencies, it should be separate and distinct from information reported on a regular basis. Responding agencies should estimate the costs and include the estimate in their reports when it exceeds $1,000.

Conclusions and Recommendations

Until now, federal evaluation practices have been characterized by an inordinate passion for methodology and technology. Both program managers and evaluation researchers have been enamored with statistics and computer capabilities. Charts, tables, and graphic equations abound, but they contribute little toward achieving national objectives. Evaluation has too often been little more than cost accounting—so many units of service rendered for so many dollars. Like management information systems, evaluation is often thought of simply in terms of an input/output process. Evaluators are unable to understand the public policy context within which evaluation must aid in increasing citizen well-being.

Although formative evaluations, which monitor ongoing programs, and summative evaluations, which assess the success of programs, have their place, they must be combined with anticipatory evaluations. This type of evaluation is vital as it forecasts the overall impact and results that a program or decision is likely to have. The Office of Technology Assessment and other executive offices such as the Department of Commerce, the Federal Energy Administration, the Department of Transportation, the National Institutes of Health, and the Department of Agriculture are directing their efforts toward providing this kind of information, but more needs to be done.

The federal government is moving closer toward the implementation of zero-base budgeting and sunset legislation. Zero-base budgeting means that every federal program would start each fiscal year

with a zero dollar base and would have to compete with other programs for a specific dollar budget. Under sunset legislation, federal
programs are given a "fixed life," and the program dies after the
specified period unless new legislation is enacted. Both activities require information on "where we have been" and "how we got
there," "where we must go" and "how we are likely to get there." In
short, evaluations must be readable, manageable, timely, and relevant if they are to help provide the answer.

10
The Case for Compensation

Introduction

Federal information demands have grown rapidly in the absence of an adequate system to assess the value and the burden of government information collections. Implementing a compensatory approach to federal data collection, through incentives offered by the familiar market mechanism of paying those who provide government with the information it requires, might place a clearly understandable dollar valuation on federal information collection activities. Information is not free, and the compensation approach recognizes that federal information requests result in real and significant costs to respondents and that agencies ought to be responsible for those costs. Information providers should be paid for furnishing information to the federal government, and federal agencies should be required to justify their information collection activities through budgetary requests.

This chapter will demonstrate that the compensatory approach to federal information collection has worked practically and has political support in Congress. Legal precedent, existing federal programs that compensate for the costs of providing information, and proposed legislation currently pending before Congress will be examined to demonstrate that compensatory information collection is a feasible approach to reducing the amount of federal paperwork.

The Debate on Compensation

Evidence disclosed by the Commission on Federal Paperwork and other officials suggests that federal officials give little attention to the significant burdens that information requests impose on respondents because the officials are not accountable for the costs and can require information free of charge. Numerous incidents suggest that the right to request information has been abused. There are cases of respondents having to provide the same or similar information to different agencies, cases in which the amount of information collected exceeds the collecting agency's ability to process it, and, finally, cases in which information is collected and coded but never used. In an attempt to curb the abuses, various clearance processes have been established, the best known of which is at the OMB. Although it is too early to say whether clearance procedures have inherent defects, since they are not comprehensive or energetically enforced, so far they have been of little value. Experience with these procedures has been sufficiently unsatisfactory to consider the need for other accountability approaches.

The introduction of the compensatory principle is perhaps the only really effective means of forcing federal officials to consider information demands more carefully than heretofore. Traditionally, the budgetary process has been one of the most effective ways of holding federal officials accountable for their activities. That process requires officials to justify their expenditures before the legislative and executive branches of government. If federal officials were required to compensate respondents for costs incurred in complying with information requests, the officials would have to justify such outlays in their budgets.

Justification of and accountability for information collection through the budgetary process would eventually take two forms: (1) an evaluation of the actual value of the information to an agency (e.g., the Tennessee Valley Authority [TVA] would be forced to evaluate the worth of knowing the number and location of electric appliances, such as toasters, within the TVA region) and (2) an evaluation of the full costs of obtaining the information, including costs that are initially borne by information providers and therefore not even calculated now, much less justified as actually necessary. If the cost of providing information were included in agency budgets, many federal agencies would find such expenditures difficult if not impossible to justify. As a consequence, federal information collection would be reduced. Compensation also would alleviate directly the costs to those who must provide the information.

In addition to efficiency, compensation payments have an "equity" component. Under current noncompensatory information collection procedures, information providers often feel exploited, harassed, "ripped-off," or deprived of something valuable without good reason or equitable treatment. Sometimes this dissatisfaction is translated into accusations of infringement of constitutional rights, such as accusations of involuntary servitude, which is forbidden by the Thirteenth Amendment, or of the taking of property without due process and without compensation proscribed by the Fifth Amendment. Although such claims would be unlikely to succeed in court, they represent real complaints about the government's enriching itself at the expense of citizens who must provide the information. Moreover, certain groups of information providers are required to shoulder more than their share of the burden of providing information to federal agencies. Federal employees, small business people, and welfare recipients are among those who complain about having to provide more than their share. By shifting some of the cost to the general tax base, the compensatory approach would partially recompense those individuals and entities that are required to provide more than their proportionate share of the information used by the federal government.

However, compensation for government information collection should not be viewed as a panacea for eliminating excessive federal information collection activities. Like all administrative tools, it has certain inherent disadvantages and potential drawbacks. The most obvious disadvantage is cost, both financial and administrative. Because government information requests have not been calculated on a comprehensive basis, it is not possible to project what the compensation would cost, and the cost would depend on the administrative procedures used. Another potential disadvantage is the possibility of information distortion, but even the voluntary approaches to information collection result in inaccuracies and distortions. It would appear that statistical systems and marketing surveys are capable of correctly adjusting for such inaccuracies no matter what system is employed.

Finally, it has been suggested that the compensatory approach might foster alienation, since the government would be paying individuals for activities they should be willing to perform as citizens. Although cooperation by the governed with their government is valuable, it should be recognized that the relationship many individuals and entities have with government is strictly on a businesslike basis; in such circumstances compensation is appropriate. Even those persons who perform such important cooperative civic duties as serving when called for jury duty are compensated, albeit nominally. In short, although alienation is a potential problem inherent in government information collection and should be guarded against, it is unlikely that alienation would be exacerbated by providing compensation for federally demanded information. On the contrary, compensation would probably help alleviate the sense of injustice and exploitation, which is a major component of alienation.

Compensation and the Law

Applying compensation to the collection of information depends ultimately upon the commonsense notion that information is something valuable for which information providers ought to be paid. As Sen. Sam J. Ervin, Jr., pointed out, information, like a commodity, "is valuable, can be bought and sold, stolen, altered, exchanged for other data and used as the basis for decision-making."[1] Just how the law would apply depends on whether the information in question would be viewed as property with inherent value or as a service that can be provided at a cost.

Because the courts and the legal scholars have been unable to reach a consensus regarding the status of information as compensable property, it is more useful to view the provision of information to the government as a service for which the providers ought to be paid.[2] The remainder of this analysis will be based on the service theory.

Why Not Cooperation Instead of Compensation?

One of the most difficult policy issues raised by the compensatory approach to government information collection concerns citizen responsibility to the government. In a democratic society, it is commonly believed that the community of the governed has substantial responsibilities for voluntarily contributing to and participating in the task of governing. The old census protest cases in 1901 discussed at length the duty of citizens to provide government with the information it seeks. The privilege is based on a broad notion of sovereignty as follows:

For the national government to know something, if not everything, beyond the fact that the population of each State reached a certain limit, is apparent, when it is considered what is the dependence of this population upon the intelligent action of the general government. Sanitation, immigration, naturalization, the opening and development of the public domain; the laying of taxes, duties, imposts and excises, involving the adjustment of duties for the purpose of revenue to the domestic products of every kind and the taxation of industries, as illustrated in the laws for collecting an internal revenue, and in what is known as the "War Revenue Tax Law;" the fostering of exports; the immense appropriation annually for the development and improvement of waterways for the purposes of commercial interchange between the States and the States and foreign nations; the establishment of post offices and post roads; the chartering of corporations for the convenient reception and distribution of money to meet the convenience and exigencies of trade; the institution of a just system of bankruptcy; the promotion of highways of travel by railway and otherwise; vigilant protection and helpful interest in suggested facilities of transportation in other countries; a judicious consideration of giving or withholding aid to our merchant marine; the necessity of providing a suitable volume of money for the purpose of facilitating the exchange of commodities; the making of commercial treaties with foreign countries and establishing reciprocal trade relations with the same; the building of ships, forts, and public buildings; the equipment and maintenance of armies, for these and similar purposes the government needs each item of information demanded by the census act, and such information, when obtained, requires the most careful study, to the end that the fulfillment of the governmental function may be wise and useful. If one shall select any of the powers reposed in the Federal Government as above indicated, and the enumeration is not complete, and consider thoughtfully the direct essential aid that the information, in whole or in part, sought by the act, must give, he will not hesitate to ascribe plenary ability to congress to obtain such information. A government whose successful maintenance depends upon the education of its citizens may not blindly legislate, but may exercise the right to proclaim its commands, after careful and full knowledge of the business life of its inhabitants, in all its intricacies and activities.[3]

The notion that government can require information from its citizens is by no means as archaic as the rhetoric of the previous case would indicate. In the most recent census protest case, the court ruled that "The authority to gather reliable statistical data reasonably related to governmental purposes and functions is a necessity if modern government is to legislate intelligently and effectively."[4] There are times when the cooperative approach to data collection works fairly well, especially in cases where government information collection provides benefits to the informers. In cases of compulsory information collection – the federal income tax forms or the disclosure and enforcement activities of the Securities and Exchange Commission – penalties for failure to provide information are deemed necessary. Here the relationship between the information provider and the government is virtually an adversary one. It has been suggested that in cases of compulsory information collection, data would be provided more readily if incentives, such as financial compensation, were offered instead of penalties.

Existing Federal Programs that Provide Compensation

A number of existing federal programs already compensate those who provide information. Two of the most interesting of these systems – the Drug Alert Warning Network (DAWN), maintained by the Drug Enforcement Administration, and the National Electronic Injury Surveillance System (NEISS), run by the Consumer Product Safety Commission – grew out of the Food and Drug Administration's program of the early 1960s.

Drug Alert Warning Network (DAWN)

The DAWN program, established in 1972, collects data about drug abuse episodes from approximately twelve hundred participating facilities comprised of hospital emergency rooms, medical examiners, and drug crisis centers. These facilities are compensated in a variety of ways for the actual total costs of filling out forms including labor, supplies, and postage. Medical examiners are paid a flat fee of $25 per month, no matter how many records they submit; hospitals are paid the exact cost of filling out each form. Basically this is a labor cost, but some hospitals have tried to include general expenses of the record-keeping section. The average cost is $1 per record, although some hospitals in major metropolitan areas have estimated the cost at $4 per record. The total cost of compensation is not available, but it is estimated to represent no more than 10 percent of the $1.7 million FDA budget for 1976. Interestingly, the FDA has not been able to satisfactorily explain or justify this compensatory program in their budgetary presentations to the OMB or Congress.

The DAWN system is considered effective by the officials who administer it. It has, however, experienced some difficulties. There are reports of inaccuracy, and officials have admitted that were compensation to cease, most reporting facilities would drop out of the system. In fact, one facility was dropped because the compensation was apparently so great an inducement that the facility manufactured nonexistent drug abuse reports. The monitoring system seems to be able to take care of the problem of fraud.

National Electronic Injury Surveillance System (NEISS)

Another computerized federal system that compensates for information is the NEISS program, established in 1970 by the FDA and, since 1973, maintained by the Consumer Product Safety Commission (CPSC), Bureau of Epidemiology. The FDA found that it needed and was not getting sufficient, accurate data on adverse drug reactions so, building on the experience of marketing surveys developed by private pharmaceutical manufacturers, it instituted this incentive, or compensatory, information collection system that pays hospitals for information supplied by them. The NEISS collects information on consumer-product-related injuries from 118 statistically selected hospitals in one of two ways: by hiring consultants to collect and code data and to conduct detailed field investigations of selected cases and by paying participating hospitals directly for information. Contractors (consultants) receive $150 for every case completed. All hospital costs are covered, and hospitals are provided with all the necessary coding and transcription equipment and trained coders and transcribers. As in the DAWN system, compensation under the NEISS program varies from provider to provider and is calculated on actual cost estimates of the man-hours needed to collect information at a particular hospital. In most cases, time studies are run on each case, and that figure is then multiplied by the hourly wage of the personnel who collect and transcribe the data. Out of a CPSC budget of $2 million, $400,000 is spent on the

NEISS program, or one-fifth of the total costs go toward information collection. The CPSC is confident that this expenditure is worthwhile and that the system provides accurate, usable data.

Intervenor Compensation Programs

One of the most innovative federal programs to compensate for the provision of information is the Federal Trade Commission's (FTC) intervenor compensation program legislated by the Magnuson-Moss Warranty-Federal Trade Commission Improvement Act of 1975. That act allows the FTC to compensate any person for reasonable costs of participation in rule-making proceedings if that person represents an interest that would not otherwise be adequately represented, if such representation is necessary for a fair determination by the agency, or if that person could not otherwise effectively afford to participate. Compensation is based on the expenses actually incurred by the intervenor, with a maximum of $50 per hour for attorneys' fees.[5]

The theory behind compensating intervenors for providing information at administrative hearings is based on the determination that some aspects of the public interest will only be effectively represented in the administrative process if the costs of participation are borne in part by the public.[6] The intent behind the FTC's intervenor compensation program is to induce participation and contribution of information from those people who are in a position to provide otherwise unavailable information and/or points of view but lack the resources to participate in a rule-making proceeding. The intervenor compensation program has worked extremely well, according to all FTC officials interviewed, with only a few administrative problems of getting compensation approved in advance of the hearing in which intervention is sought.

Nuclear Regulatory Commission (NRC)

The most useful and comprehensive discussion of the intervenor compensation concept is contained in a report to the Nuclear Regulatory Commission (NRC) entitled "Policy Issues Raised by Intervenor Requests for Financial Assistance in NRC Proceedings" (1975). It debates the arguments for and against adopting such a compensatory approach and presents the following arguments in support of compensation.

1. Intervenors can make significant contributions to the hearing process.
2. Intervenors serve as gadflies to the staffs and boards.
3. Funding will increase the public's education and confidence in the agency.
4. All information affecting health, safety, economic, and environmental factors of a decision should be thoroughly reviewed.

Arguments against compensation are also presented.

1. The program is expensive and causes delays and various administrative difficulties.
2. It results in duplication, since the agency already represents the public interest.
3. It interjects an adversary attitude and process into the search for technological truth.

In discussing previous efforts to determine the amount of compensation to be paid to intervenors in the administrative process, the report summarizes existing federal statutes that authorize compensation for attorneys' fees and other costs. Of the forty-eight statutes, a number concern public interest groups, the most prominent of which is the Consumers Union. Most of the groups take the position that the agencies' general regulatory powers already empower federal agencies to compensate intervenors who provide information through the administrative process.

Government Procurement Practices

A review of government procurement practices raises interesting questions concerning what constitutes appropriate precedents. The federal government spends approximately $200 million a year for information in the form of program evaluations, it pays "hardware" contractors for feasibility studies and for technical descriptions of hardware they sell to the government, and it pays commercial firms (about $100 million a year) for surveys. Only recently has the government begun to compensate third parties for providing information in response to federal agency summonses. The Tax Reform Act of 1976 allows the reimbursement of the following fees and costs to witnesses who testify before the Internal Revenue Service (IRS): (1) fees and mileage to persons who are summoned to appear before the secretary and (2) such costs that are reasonably necessary and have been directly incurred in searching for, reproducing, or transporting books, papers, records, or other data required to be produced by summons.[7]

Under the federal courts' general equitable powers, a number of courts have awarded compensation to banks that comply with IRS administrative summonses. The Friedman case is particularly interesting because it reviews the compensation issue and contains a survey of the costs involved in responding to an IRS summons (see Table 10.1).[8] The survey suggests eight factors that affect the cost of providing information about customer records in response to IRS administrative summonses.

1. The size of the bank, i.e., level of deposits
2. The nature of the bank's business, i.e., whether it emphasizes retail, consumer, or wholesale banking
3. The number and type of individual and business accounts and banking services that the bank offers to the public
4. The economic character and size of the geographic area in which the bank maintains banking facilities
5. The number and location of the bank's branches
6. The methods the bank uses to keep customer records, i.e., a centralized records system, a noncentralized system, a fully or partially automated system, or a manual records system
7. The number and capabilities of personnel who process IRS requests, including access to legal counsel for summons review
8. The number of IRS administrative summonses received each year, which will be variously affected by factors one through five

The banking industry has been willing to absorb some of the costs as

Table 10.1

American Bankers Association Survey of the Costs in Responding

to an IRS Summons

Bank	Deposit Range (In Billions)	Annual Number of Summonses	Average Cost Per Summons	Estimated Annual Cost
A**	1-5	350	$230.00	$ 80,500.00
B**	10-20	1,240	$118.00	$146,320.00
C*	1-5	15	$ 20.00	300.00
D***	Under 1	25	$160.00	$ 4,000.00
E**	1-5	40	$229.00	$ 9,160.00
F***	5-10	300	$140.00	$ 42,000.00
G**	over 20	4,000	$220.00	- -
H**	over 20	1,619	$151.56	$245,375.64
I**	1-5	96	$100.00	$ 9,600.00
J***	10-20	1,800	$274.85	$494,730.00
K**	1-5	200	$354.99	$ 70,998.00
L***	10-20	1,000	$300.00	$300,000.00
M**	1-5	120	$175.00	$ 21,000.00
N***	1-5	300	$200.00	$ 60,000.00
O***	over 20	2,040	$250.00	$510,000.00
P*	10-20	212	$225.00	$ 47,700.00
Q**	1-5	90	$175.00	$ 15,750.00
R**	1-5	75	$200.00	$ 15,000.00
S**	1-5	100	$220.00	$ 22,000.00
T***	10-20	1,000	$175.00	$175,000.00
U**	over 20	400	$200.00	$ 80,000.00
V**	5-10	212	$275.00	$ 58,300.00

KEY
 *branches prohibited
 **limited area branching
***statewide branching

Source: U.S. v. Friedman, 388 F. Supp. 963 (W. D. Pa. 1975).

part of overhead expenses. But when the cost of providing information to the government reaches what is considered to be an inequi-
table burden on a particular bank (e.g., $3,000 to $5,000 for responding to some IRS summonses in criminal fraud cases), then the
courts have agreed with the banks that compensation is warranted.

Of interest to all federal agencies, there is a significant piece of legislation pending in Congress relating to compensation for information provided by individuals and entities to the federal government.[9]
The proposed legislation provides for direct tax credits to individu-

als calculated on a sliding scale granting the largest tax credit to the most exploited information providers on the following basis: (1) individuals—ten cents per item of information or inquiry, but not less than one dollar for each form or document; (2) corporations (exclusive of small businesses) and state or local governments—twenty cents per item of information or inquiry, but not less than two dollars for each form or document; and (3) small businesses—thirty cents per item of information or inquiry, but not less than three dollars for each form or document. The tax credit mechanism was chosen for all cases (except state and local governments for which direct payments are provided) because it is easy to administer and it keeps the finance committee's jurisdiction over the legislation. The compensation amounts were determined arbitrarily, in an effort to provide for compensation of actual costs without having to calculate exact figures.

The intent of the legislation is to deter useless information collection by federal agencies. However, because compensation would be paid through a tax rebate, the attendant information costs would not be subject to an annual budgetary review. In short, the proposed legislation satisfies the equity criterion but largely fails to satisfy the accountability criterion.

Finally, there is a broad range of legislative proposals that would extend compensation to those people who participate in federal administrative or judicial proceedings. The most controversial, and the most likely to be enacted, is the "Public Participation in Government Proceedings Act" of 1976.[10] Based on the FTC's intervenor compensation program discussed above, the bill proposes an extension of the compensatory approach to all federal agencies subject to the Administrative Procedures Act, provided that

1. the view of the public participant prevails,
2. the award of costs serves a public purpose,
3. the intervenor does not stand to gain a substantial profit, and
4. the intervenor does not otherwise have sufficient resources to participate effectively.

The intent behind the proposal is to induce participation in the administrative process by public-interest advocates, who would be unable to supply information and perspectives important to administrative decision making without this incentive. It is an attempt "to restore some balance between those representing special interests and the general public in their access to the Federal administrative process. If this goal can be achieved, not only will the public be well served, but the agencies themselves will greatly benefit from the increased contributions by public groups."[11]

During hearings held by the Senate Judiciary Subcommittee on Administrative Practices and Procedures, an attempt was made to estimate the costs involved in implementing such a compensatory system. Based on a Congressional Research Service survey of cases in which compensation has been awarded by the courts, the subcommittee estimated that the expenditure level for intervenor compensation under the proposed legislation would cost less than $13 million per year.[12]

Other related, but conceptually different, legislative proposals would provide compensation to parties involved in litigation or administrative proceedings with the federal government.[13] The general aim of those proposals is to deter federal agencies from initiating some unnecessary judicial or administrative proceedings by making the agencies liable for the costs.

Conclusions

Compensation for information appears to be a conceptually sound idea for reducing burgeoning federal paperwork excesses. It would induce greater efficiency in federal agency information collection by forcing a recognition of the costs involved and, at the same time, offer information providers more equitable treatment by the government. Potential problems of cost, accuracy, and alienation appear to be soluble. Moreover, the quality of information collected when compensation is provided, on a service-rendered basis, has been demonstrated by legal precedent and by several successful federal programs.

It appears that the time has come for compensation for information. There is considerable political interest in the idea as the variety of legislative proposals currently pending before Congress demonstrates. It is recommended that several kinds of pilot compensation-for-information programs be undertaken to reduce the aggregate volume of federal paperwork and to treat in a more

equitable fashion those who are burdened with providing information to the federal government. One type of pilot program might be
based in a federal agency, and the criteria for selecting a particular
agency or area should include consideration of (1) where government information collection imposes a significant burden, (2) where
the information provision burden falls particularly heavily on one
type of activity or information provider, (3) where the information
provider does not receive any direct reciprocal benefits from the information system, and (4) where there is no statutory requirement
that the information be provided.

Another, more novel, pilot program would be broadly applicable
to all citizens. General legislation would be passed, classifying allowable areas of and limits to federal information requests. When either
the allowable areas or limits were exceeded by federal requests,
respondents could press claims against the government for compensation. The courts would handle the claims directly or develop an
intermediate administrative tribunal, perhaps connected with the
Federal Reports Act, to pass upon the merits of a case and make a
judgment.

Although compensation is no panacea for eliminating excessive
federal information gathering activities, it can be an effective tool in
reducing the direct financial and psychological burdens associated
with federal paperwork. It should be tried.

11
Conclusions:
Recommendations and an
Agenda for Future Research

The chapters in this book have (a) assessed the root causes under-lying the values and burdens of information acquisition, processing, and application by the U.S. federal government; (b) provided a framework for analyzing effective and efficient government informa-tion practices through the value/burden technique and comparative agency analyses; and (c) described some techniques for identifying problem areas in order to eliminate some of the problems. We view the material presented as being an exploratory, first look at each of the three areas.

The burdens and values related to federal information manage-ment practices cannot be expressed simply in terms of "exclusive" or "appropriate" requirements for information from federal, state, and local institutions. "Burden" and "value" may be expressed directly in terms of information management practices that increase or decrease the probability of excessive paperwork requirements. The direct burdens and excesses are the easiest to identify.

There is, however, an expansion of some generally accepted gov-ernment practices that indirectly, but significantly, affect the poten-tial for establishing practices and procedures that increase citizen well-being (value). For example, as indicated in Chapter 2, bureau-crats select information to be passed on to their superiors by criteria other than quality and objectivity. As a result, they may order ex-cessive amounts of information to be collected in order to find re-sults that are "politically acceptable." Similarly, as highlighted in Chapters 2 and 3, there is an underlying incentive system at the federal level that rewards inefficient practices. Efficiency is not the major criterion of accountability; instead, loyalty to one's organization and the ideology of that organization (i.e., autonomy, discretion, power) are the primary criteria by which individual and organizational practices are judged.

It would be natural to simply assign to the OMB responsibility for implementing any recommendations related to federal information management. Before doing this, however, it is important to analyze past successes and failures of the OMB and the reasons for them. Particular attention should be given to determining to what extent agency/department unwillingness to be managed by inadequate/incompetent personnel within the OMB has been a primary reason for past failures.

Moreover, we strongly feel that the OMB should not be primarily responsible for information management. The White House should recommend that both the value/burden calculus and the comparative agency analysis techniques be considered by the appropriate assistant secretaries in the federal agencies as ways to streamline their information practices to make them more effective.

Recommendations

A. National Priorities

The poor articulation of national objectives leads to uncertainty and misunderstandings about the appropriate roles of federal agencies. A White House unit, the Congressional Budget Office, and two or three private groups with national reputations that are known to have different political views should enter into a continuing exercise to set national goals and to establish national priorities. Such an exercise would provide a framework against which to assess what information is of value to the government and would be a means of increasing citizen well-being. From these discussions an implementation plan should be developed that would spell out budgetary allocations and agency/departmental responsibilities for attaining the goals of the plan. The results of this continual exercise should be reported on an annual basis in a document similar to the *Economic Report of the President*. This document should show, in quantitative terms, wherever possible, how the activities of each federal government entity are contributing to the attainment of the national objectives.

B. Incentives and Bureaucratic/Political Dynamics

We strongly believe that the underlying incentive system within the federal government contributes directly to excessive paperwork and to inefficient management, both of which decrease the potential to realize "value." Along these lines, the federal government has made some efforts to increase efficiency and at the same time reduce direct burdens on the public at large as well as on public and private institutions. These efforts include supporting (1) sunset legislation — aimed at reviewing programs and challenging the assumption that "they will always be there"; (2) zero-base budgeting — aimed in particular at challenging the assumption that funds will always be increasing; and (3) management by objectives — aimed at gaining organizational concensus on working goals.

There is no doubt that these efforts to increase efficiency may involve sustained paperwork requirements that would not have been present under the "old system." However, these requirements (potential burdens) need to be measured against their added value. On balance we believe that value is added through each of these measures.

However, each of these programs/techniques only treats the symptoms of direct and indirect burdens, not their causes. Measures need to be adopted that will address the foundation of the current incentive system. President Carter has attempted to do this, in part, through the Civil Service Reform Legislation of 1978. Broadly, he is trying to establish

- differential rewards — civil servants would be singled out for especially desirable behavior;
- a system of special cash bonuses — to be awarded at any time during the year;
- more flexibility in promotion;
- legitimate communication channels for formal dissent.

Clearly, these measures were designed with an awareness of the

typical bureaucratic pathologies discussed in Chapter 2. The success of these types of measures, however, depends upon the executive branch's ability to specify what types of behavior are to be rewarded and to monitor the process that determines the awards to
be given. It is simply not sufficient "to put the bureaucrats on
notice"; they must be convinced that their regular and established
practices are no longer operable. If they cannot be convinced of this
fact, the new measures will be interpreted as symbolic only, and
they will be ignored in practice.

Specifically, we feel that there are four main types of behavior
that should be rewarded. The first type is for the sharing of information at the inter- and intra-organizational levels. Similarly, withholding of information for other than national security reasons should be
openly reprimanded. Second, information gathering and application
that involve more than one agency should be coordinated. This becomes particularly important as substantive policy areas become
more complex and require expertise from more than one agency. In
the absence of this type of coordination, one can expect the production of excessive paperwork in the form of duplication and repeti-
tion. Third, rewards should be given to bureaucrats who are instrumental in rejecting information requests that will burden the public
and/or not lead to citizens' well-being. Fourth, bureaucrats who
alter or distort information should be openly reprimanded. These
are some of the specific types of guidelines that have potential for
changing the current incentive system within the federal government.

C. *The Value/Burden Calculus*

As already indicated at the beginning of this chapter, we feel that
it is important for the assistant secretaries to give careful consideration to using the value/burden calculus to help attain efficient and
effective information management, and some rather elementary
rules should be followed. First, information requests that have more
burden than value should be rejected. Second, during the acquisition, processing, and application of information, the potential for
burden should be monitored. When it becomes clear that an information request is becoming burdensome, it should be terminated.
Third, either the requirement to report respondent burden data
should be dropped or OMB practices should be changed. Specifi-

cally, the burden data will not be useful until it is made accurate, until it includes psychological burdens, and until the clearance process is made comprehensive both in terms of requiring clearance on all forms and in terms of covering all agencies now reporting to the General Accounting Office. The resulting figures should be analyzed with the aim of developing criteria for the appropriate burden levels for different agencies. Next, government data collection instruments that require the collection of information only on a voluntary basis should not have to go through the OMB clearance process. In addition, "utilization" should be dropped as the primary criterion for judging value. Instead, measures should be adopted (and legislatively mandated) that document the degree to which information collection and application are related to the realization of national objectives. Last, both direct and indirect value should become primary factors in the OMB and GAO clearance procedures.

D. Comparative Agency Analysis

Along with the value/burden calculus, we recommend that the comparative agency analysis technique be used by the assistant secretaries responsible for information management. If effective information management practices are to be developed, then it is essential that agency activities — especially those of regulatory agencies — be examined and compared as to the development, implementation, evaluation, and monitoring of rules and standards.

The comparative agency analysis is offered as a way of clarifying the key questions that should be addressed. For example, the standard approval procedures of the FMC and the ICC should be reviewed with the aim of increasing clarity and federal discretion in other regulatory commissions. Clarity in the development and implementation of standards appears to be strongly correlated with efficiency.

Similarly, the monitoring and enforcement activities of the CAB should be compared with those of the FDA. The former can be classified as preventative and the latter as punitive. The CAB is concerned with monitoring before a violation occurs, and the FDA concentrates on locating and prosecuting those who have already violated the law. It is not necessarily clear which approach is more effective and/or less paperwork intensive. However, it is very clear that agency practices need to be compared so that regulatory practices can be improved and citizen well-being increased.

*E. Techniques for Information Management
and Assessing Efficiency*

1. *Management Information Systems.* Several specific recommendations concerning management information systems can be followed. First, value/burden assessments of selected information
from large-scale and smaller-sized information systems should be
conducted. Second, after the value/burden assessments have been
completed, further work is needed to ensure that (a) systems are designed on the basis of users' needs rather than systems technology
and (b) experience with successful systems is transmitted to other
agencies and programs contemplating the development or expansion
of large-scale systems.

Third, differences in the technical capabilities of potential and actual providers of "data" to the systems should be identified and considered when decisions are made to collect the information or to
compensate respondents for providing the information required.
Fourth, equality of access to government information requires that
the technical capabilities of potential government and nongovernment users should be identified and considered when decisions to
collect information are made.

2. *Evaluation.* Program evaluation is an important and useful tool
for increasing the efficiency and the effectiveness of the federal
government. In order to contribute to a positive value/burden
assessment, the following recommendations are made. One, federal
executive agencies and the GAO should set aside funds to determine the effects general purpose programs are having on specific
social objectives as mandated by Congress and the executive
branch. These studies should also address the problem of how the
information for the specific evaluations can be integrated into more
comprehensive evaluation activities.

Two, the primary emphasis of evaluation activity within the federal government should be changed. Instead of focusing on ex post
facto summative grading exercises, attention should be directed to
ongoing evaluations conducted at various points throughout the lifetime of a project. These evaluations should offer diagnostic and prescriptive information that sets forth what can be done to eliminate
or ameliorate problems before or as they occur. The evaluations

should also measure the success and/or failure of projects.

Three, as already noted, the basic evaluation pattern rests on comparing the present state of goals indicators with the ideal set (or expected progress toward a goal). The legislation calling for evaluation should be made more specific, and assistant secretaries of policy, planning, and evaluation should be required to report to Congress on the relationship between evaluations and national goals and priorities. These reports would be made in open hearings.

Four, if the implementation of programs is to be effective at the local and state levels and if evaluations are to provide decision makers with ongoing data to monitor progress, then effective feedback systems must be designed to serve local, state, and federal audiences. Contracting offices should stipulate, as part of the original contract, the number of reports that must be made to the states and localities.

Five, if policymaking practices are to be effective, evaluations that are anticipatory in nature must be made. Contracting offices should stipulate that the probable consequences of the programs under consideration should be analyzed. Policymakers should have this type of information before a final decision must be made.

3. *Compensation.* In terms of dealing directly with the burden of federal information requirements, we have discussed the notion of direct compensation. Our analysis leads to the recommendation that when the information burden on a firm, institution, or individual—as measured by man-hour wage equivalents—exceeds 1 percent of total sales or gross income of the firm or individual, every additional man-hour input should be compensated for by the federal government on a five-dollars-per-hour basis.

F. Future Research Agenda

The general, substantive recommendations offered thus far reflect the current "state of the art" of information management. Very little analysis of the techniques of information management has been completed and still less has been experimented with. In terms of future substantive research, the following guidelines would serve as a logical extension of our analysis.

The Value/Burden Calculus. First, the National Science Foundation (or some other appropriate funding agency) should sponsor a study on the measurement of value and burden. This work should not be conceptual but should entail developing specific instruments to measure value and burden. It should also involve experimentation (administrative experiments) with various measurement techniques. Second, research should also be funded that is aimed at continuing to identify and measure the psychological burdens associated with information reporting.

Comparative Administrative Practices. One, the National Science Foundation (or some other appropriate government funding agency) should be asked to fund a study of comparative federal agency information practices. Some of the specific areas for comparative case studies should include information activities associated with problem design, program implementation, program monitoring and evaluation, and program redesign and replication. Two, agencies should fund administrative experiments designed to test the effectiveness of techniques to increase the efficiency and effectiveness of federal agencies.

It is conceivable that a special interagency coordinating task force should be established to examine and compare federal agency activities. In the past, interagency task forces have been successful in coordinating activities that have been designated as priority issues at the highest levels of government.

General Philosophy

In general, we feel that we have developed a framework for effective information management—the value/burden calculus and the comparative agency analysis. This framework now needs to be employed to complete an in-depth analysis of the dimensions of the information management problem that have only been introduced in this counter-report. Such studies, however, should lead to the identification and specification of management techniques that can be employed by government officials.

Agencies should be encouraged to experiment with techniques to reduce information burdens and increase the effectiveness and efficiency of government practices. Until the government feels confident that it has developed a portfolio of techniques that can be used in the government as a whole, it would be advisable to coordinate the experiments and employ an overall quasi-experimental design. Agencies with similar functions (and legislative mandates) can experiment with different techniques aimed at achieving the same objective, effective and efficient information management. This process could be continued in cycles until a useful portfolio of techniques has been developed.

Given that this type of experimentation is not consistent with regular operating practices and procedures at the federal level, legislative mandates should be provided. Mandates would have the effect of committing both the legislative branch and the executive branch to the same overall objective. This history of both branches of the federal government points to the need for involving both of them in the process of improving information management at the federal level.

Epilogue

As we have emphasized throughout this book, bureaucratic and political dynamics lie at the heart of information management problems in the federal government. Finding long-lasting and effective counter-incentives to deal with these problems is perhaps beyond our capabilities. In any case, the potential intractability of the problems should be recognized in the rush to find quick solutions.

We have characterized the federal government as a grouping of competitive organizations in which unshared information is valuable. This undoubtedly results in some redundancy, but probably some competition is good and some redundancy should be tolerated. After all, in the private sector, the sharing of information is discouraged by the antitrust laws, and secrets are allowed to be kept by the patent laws—all for the sake of competition.

Given the potential intractability of the problems and the desirability of some interagency competition, some information excesses should be tolerated. Perhaps information management efforts should devote greater attention to ensuring that government officials have access to information and give greater attention to the information that is most relevant to the policy matters at hand.

Notes

Chapter 1

1. Marc Uri Porat, *The Information Economy*, vol. 1 (Stanford, Calif.: Stanford University Press, 1976).
2. The agencies cited are EPA versus ICC, CAB, and FMC.
3. The agencies cited are ICC, FMC, CAB, and SEC versus FDA and FCC.
4. The agencies cited are FMC, and ICC versus OSHA and FDA.

Chapter 2

1. J. A. Stockfish, "The Bureaucratic Pathology," in *Federal Statistics: Report of the President's Commission,* 2 vols. (Washington, D.C.: U.S. Government Printing Office, 1971), 2:459.
2. S. N. Eisenstadt, *The Political System of Empires* (New York: Free Press, 1969), p. 160.
3. Max Weber, *Economy and Society*, ed. Guenther Roth and Claus Wittich (New York: Bedminister Press, 1968), 3:973–74.
4. Ibid., pp. 1393 ff.
5. Ibid.
6. Ibid., p. 1418.
7. *Federal Statistics: Report of the President's Commission,* 2 vols. (Washington, D.C.: U.S. Government Printing Office, 1971), 1:89–90.
8. Daniel P. Moynihan, *Coping* (New York: Random House, 1973), pp. 272–73.
9. Ibid., p. 274.
10. Ibid., p. 276.

11. Reinhard Bendix, "Bureaucracy," *International Encyclopedia of the Social Sciences* (New York: Macmillan, 1970), 2:213.

12. Stockfish, "The Bureaucratic Pathology," p. 460.

13. Arthur Schlesinger, *The Imperial Presidency* (Boston: Houghton Mifflin Company, 1973), pp. 332–33.

14. Ibid., p. 337.

15. Weber, *Economy and Society*, p. 992.

16. Schlesinger, *Imperial Presidency*, entire chapter on secrecy.

17. N. Caplan and R. F. Rich, "Open and Closed Knowledge Inquiry Systems: the Process and Consequences of Bureaucratization of Information Policy at the National Level" (Paper presented at the OECD Conference on Dissemination of Economic and Social Development Research Results, Bogotá, Colombia, June 1976).

18. For a thorough analysis of the appointment criteria for high-level bureaucrats and political executives, see Hugh Heclo, *A Government of Strangers* (Washington, D.C.: Brookings Institution, 1977).

19. Irving Louis Horowitz, *The Rise and Fall of Project Camelot* (Cambridge, Mass.: M.I.T. Press, 1967), p. 20.

20. Morton H. Halperin, *Bureaucratic Politics and Foreign Policy* (Washington, D.C.: Brookings Institution, 1974), p. 36.

21. Michael A. Michaud, "Communications and Controversy: Thoughts on the Future of Foreign Service Reporting," *Foreign Service Journal* (October 1968), p. 148.

22. Ibid.

23. Richard Rose, in *Social Policies and Indicators* (New York: Social Science Research Council, 1973), p. 134.

24. Ibid.

25. Harold Wilensky, *Organizational Intelligence* (New York: Basic Books, 1967), p. 77. This is representative of a common theme in the literature on organizations.

26. Robert A. Levine, *Public Planning: Failure and Redirection* (New York: Basic Books, 1972), p. 149.

27. N. Caplan, A. Morrison, and R. J. Stambaugh, *The Use of Social Science Knowledge in Policy Decisions at the National Level* (Ann Arbor: Institute for Social Research, 1975), pp. 83–84.

28. Kenneth Arrow, *The Limits of Organization,* (New York: W. W. Norton and Company, 1974), pp. 39, 41.

29. Anthony Downs, *Economic Theory of Democracy* (New York: Harper and Row, 1957), p. 24.

30. Warren Ilchman and Norman Uphoff, *The Political Economy of Change* (Berkeley: University of California Press, 1971), p. 68.

31. Downs, *Economic Theory*, p. 207.

32. Warren Ilchman, "Measure for Measure: Administrative Productivity in the Second Development Decade" (Paper for a panel seminar, March 1973), pp. 25–27.

33. M. Sackman and Norman Nie, *The Information Utility of Social Choice* (Montvale, N.J.: A.F.I.P.S. Press, 1970), p. 194.

34. Phillip M. Hauser, "Statistics and Politics" (Paper prepared for the Annual Meeting of the American Statistical Association, August 15, 1972), p. 11.

35. John Sibley, "Student Says a Policeman Tried to Falsify a Report of a Holdup," *New York Times,* November 23, 1972, pp. 5, 40.

36. Donald T. Campbell, "Administrative Experiments, Institutional Records, and Non-Reactive Measures," in William Evans, ed., *Organizational Experiments* (New York: Harper and Row, 1971), p. 178.

37. Andrew Gordon et al., "Public Access to Information," *Northwestern Law Review* 68, no. 2 (May/June 1973), pp. 285–86.

38. Ibid., p. 294.

39. Donald T. Campbell, "The Experimenting Society" (Address given to the American Psychological Association, September 1972), p. 29.

40. Halperin, *Bureaucratic Politics,* p. 159.

41. Alexander L. George, "The Case for Multiple Advocacy in Making Foreign Policy," *American Political Science Review* 66 (September 1972), p. 777.

42. Ibid.

43. Ibid., p. 775.

44. Ibid.

45. Luigi Einaudi, *Assistance to Peru: A Case Study, 1963–8* (Santa Monica, Calif.: RAND Corporation, 1974), pp. 37–38.

46. Henry A. Kissinger, "Bureaucracy and Policy-Making: The Effect of Insiders and Outsiders on the Policy Process," in Morton H. Halperin and Arnold Kanter, eds . *Readings in Ameican Foreign Policy: A Bureaucratic Perspective* (Boston: Little, Brown & Co., 1973), p. 91.

47. Henry A. Kissinger, *American Foreign Policy* (New York: W. W. Norton, 1961), p. 8.

48. Henry A. Kissinger quoted in Ray S. Cline, "Policy Without Intelligence," *Foreign Policy* no. 17 (Winter 1974–75), p. 123.

Chapter 3

1. "Reduction in Reports Required of the American Public" (memorandum for the heads of the departments and agencies, February 16, 1977).

2. For further details on this clearance process, see Chapter 5 on burden estimation techniques.

3. Letter, Comptroller General Staats to Sen. Lee Metcalf, January 6, 1976.

4. U.S., Congress, Joint Committee on Congressional Operations, *Hearings on Congressional Research Support and Information Services,* 93rd Cong., 2nd sess., June 19, 1974, p. 123.

5. For further details, see Chapter 8 on management information systems.

Chapter 4

1. Daniel Bell, *The Coming of Post-Industrial Society* (New York: Basic Books, 1974), p. 212.

2. Ibid., pp. 250–51.

3. It should be clear from the outset that this chapter is not addressing the traditional epistemological questions related to the place of human values and value judgments within the process of scientific inquiry. It is assumed that value judgments are faced in all phases of policy deliberation. Although an important topic for research, it is not at the core of this chapter.

4. See the National Academy of Sciences, *The Federal Investment in Knowledge of Social Problems,* Study project on social research and development, National Research Council (Washington, D.C., 1978). Within this context it should be noted that 12 percent of the dollars spent on social R&D are spent at the federal level on policy formulation. However, specifying value for activities related to federal policy formulation probably represents the most difficult and important task to be faced. Other standard statistical procedures and routine reporting requirements are related to more mechnical/technical problems.

5. Within this context, it should also be noted that the definition of citizen well-being does not make any assumptions about the distribution of benefits across society.

6. See N. Caplan and E. Barton, *Social Indicators '73: A Study of the Relationship Between the Power of Information and Utilization by Federal Executives* (Ann Arbor, Mich.: Institute for Social Research, 1976), for further details.

7. See R. F. Rich, *The Power of Information for Federal Bureaucrats* (San Francisco: Jossey-Bass, 1980).

8. For further details, see N. Caplan, A. Morrison, and R. J. Stambaugh, *The Use of Social Science Knowledge in Policy Decisions at the National Level* (Ann Arbor, Mich.: Institute for Social Research, 1975).

9. See Carol Weiss, "Research for Policy's Sake" (Address given at Case Western Reserve University, 1976).

10. See Ronald Havelock, "Highway Safety Research Communications: Is There a System?" *Institute for Social Research, CRUSK* (March 1973).

11. See Gerald E. Calderone, *Statistics About Society: The Production and Use of Federal Data* (Beverly Hills, Calif.: Sage Publications, 1974), for this type of budgetary analysis.

12. See Jack Walker, "Innovation in State's Politics," in Herbert Jacob and Kenneth N. Vines, eds. *Politics in the American States* (Boston: Little, Brown & Co., 1971).

13. R. F. Rich and N. Caplan, "Policy Uses of Social Science Knowledge and Perspectives: Means/Ends Matching vs. Understanding" (Paper presented at the OECD Conference on Dissemination of Economic and Social Development Research Results, Bogotá, Colombia, June 1976).

14. Ibid.

15. Rich, *Power of Information*.

Chapter 5

1. "Project," *Michigan Law Review* 73, no. 971 (May/June 1975), p. 1227.

2. Gordon Taichet, president of Buckeye Feed and Supply, Inc., and Max Weil, Max Weil Associates (Chicago, Commission on Federal Paperwork Hearing, June 1976).

3. Gerald Thorton, general counsel and vice-president of Administrative Services (Chicago, Commission on Federal Paperwork Hearing, June 1976).

4. Ashley De Shazor, corporate manager, vice-president, Consumer Credit, Montgomery Ward and Co., Chicago, Ill. (Chicago, Commission on Federal Paperwork Hearing, February 1977).

5. Don Loftus, general manager for government and urban affairs for the Indianapolis Chamber of Commerce (Lafayette, Commission on Federal Paperwork Hearing, June 1976).

6. Mr. Howard Weston, vice-president and manager of Installment Loan Department, Washington Trust Company (Washington, D.C., Commission on Federal Paperwork Hearing, June 1976).

7. Christopher Pyle, *Surveillance and Espionage in a Free Society*, Testimony presented at the Joint Hearings on Privacy of the Senate Committee on Government Operations and the Senate Judiciary Committee, 93rd Cong., 2d sess., June 18–20, 1974, pp. 105–11.

8. Cornelius Gallagher, "Privacy, Human Values, and Democratic Institutions," *Computers and Automation* (October 1971), pp. 46–47.

9. Chicago, Commission on Federal Paperwork Hearing, June 1976.

10. Letter, Maple Crude Oil Purchasing Company to the Federal

Energy Administration, April 8, 1976.

   11. Chicago, Commission on Federal Paperwork Hearing, June 1976.

Chapter 6

   1. For a detailed discussion of the relationship between staff professional background and the type of decision criteria employed by an agency,
see Chapter 2.

Chapter 7

   1. Except in the enforcement section, no distinction is made between
air- and water-quality programs within EPA due to their generally parallel
program designs and structures.

   2. The National Electronic Injury Surveillance System (NEISS) gathers
injury data from a statistical sample of hospital emergency rooms.

   3. This is tantamount to approving the sale of corporate securities.

   4. At the time of the Food Additive Amendment of 1958 and the Color
Additive Amendment of 1960, some 675 food substances were recognized
as safe by the industry and were not subject to premarket approval.
However, the FDA continues to conduct and monitor their safety and can
remove them from the market if they are later proven to be unsafe. For example, in 1976 FD&C Red No. 2 was banned after having been on the
market for over sixty-eight years.

   5. These exemptions are: (1) private offerings to a limited number of persons or institutions who have access to the kind of information that
registration would disclose and who do not propose to redistribute the
securities; (2) offerings restricted to the residents of the state in which the
issuing company is organized and doing business; (3) securities of
municipal, state, federal, and other government instrumentalities, of
charitable institutions, of banks, and of carriers subject to the Interstate
Commerce Act; (4) offerings not in excess of certain specified amounts
made in compliance with regulations of the commission; and (5) offerings of
"small business investment companies" made in accordance with rules and
regulations of the commission. The antifraud provisions, however, apply
to all sales of securities involving interstate commerce or the mails,
whether or not the securities are exempt from registration.

   6. Licenses are granted for a period of three years and then a renewal
application must be filed.

   7. Normally the number of petitions received per year requires twice
that amount.

8. No cost breakdown was available. An approved registration statement is good for sixteen months and then must be updated, submitted, and approved.

9. An applicant must have sufficient liquid assets to operate the station for one year without the need for any cash flow from the station itself.

10. The applicant may also appeal the changes to the commission or withdraw the statement.

11. For the purpose of this study the assumption is accepted that rate regulation is warranted. However, in carrying out the study, numerous cases were found in which regulatory activities have been carried to absurd extremes. For a discussion of what role regulation should play, see U.S., Department of Commerce, *Toward Regulatory Reasonableness* (Washington, D.C.: U.S. Government Printing Office, 1977).

12. Rules pertaining to procedural considerations of tariff proposals, such as typing format or inclusion of supportive data, are stated clearly. Substantive rules such as what constitutes an acceptable rate are not very precise, and this study concerns, for the most part, substantive rules.

13. It is uncertain whether this rate should be considered an average or a ceiling.

Chapter 8

1. There is a fundamental difference between data and information. Data are collections of signs and characters generally arranged in some orderly way to represent facts. Information represents data evaluated for its worth to a specific individual in a specific situation for a specific use. The value of information is not detached and permanent in itself. Its value is a function of several properties that determine its utility and its utilization. Data can be stored and inventoried, but information is a perishable commodity.

Chapter 9

1. See, for example, Henry W. Rieken and Robert F. Boruch, *Social Experimentation: A Method for Planning and Evaluating Social Interventions* (New York: Academic Press, 1974), pp. 239–44.

2. Donald T. Campbell, "The Experimenting Society" (Address given to the American Psychological Association, September 1972).

3. Ilene Bernstein and Howard Freeman, *Academic Entrepreneurship* (New York: Russell Sage Foundation, 1976).

4. David K. Cohen, "Politics and Research: Evaluation of Social Action

Programs in Education," in Carol H. Weiss, ed., *Evaluating Action Programs* (Boston: Allyn and Bacon, 1972), p. 39.

5. Donald T. Campbell, "Reforms as Experiments," *American Psychologist* 24, no. 4 (April 1969), p. 412.

Chapter 10

1. *Hearings on Privacy: The Collection, Use, and Computerization of Personal Data,* held jointly before the Senate Government Operations Ad Hoc Subcommittee on Privacy and Information Systems and the Senate Judiciary Subcommittee on Constitutional Rights, 93rd Cong., 2d sess., June 18–20, 1974.

2. For further discussion of information as a service, see International News Service v. Associated Press, 39 Sp. Ct. 68 (1918); U.S. v. Bottone, 365 F. 2d 389 (2d Cir. 1966) cert. denied, 385 U.S. 974 (1966); and U.S. v. DiGilio, (3d Cir. 1976) 45 *U.S. Law Week* 2002.

3. U.S. v. Moriarity, 106 F. 886, 891 (N.Y. Cir. 1901).

4. U.S. v. Rickenbacker, 309 F. 2d 462 (2d Cir. 1962) cert. denied, 83 Sp. Ct. 542 (1963).

5. The FTC's proposed regulations for the intervenor compensation program are published by the *Federal Register* 40 (April 4, 1975), p. 15238.

6. See S. Lazarus and J. Onek, "The Regulators and the People," *Virginia Law Review* 57 (1971), p. 1069.

7. Tax Reform Act of 1976, Section 7610.

8. U.S. v. Friedman, 388 F. Supp. 963 (W.D. Pa. 1975), recently affirmed by the Third Circuit Court of Appeals.

9. The Senate bill, S. 2814, was introduced by Senator Long in 1976; the House bill, H.R. 11983, was introduced by Representative Lujan in the same year.

10. The Senate bill, S. 2715, was introduced by Senator E. Kennedy; the House bill, H.R. 13901, was introduced by Representative Rodino.

11. Hearings before the Senate Judiciary Subcommittee on Administrative Practices and Procedures on the Public Participation Act of 1976, 94th Cong., 2d sess., no. 94 at 863.

12. Ibid.

13. They include the following bills: S. Res. 2871 introduced by Senator Buckley; H.R. 12812 and H.R. 4476, introduced by representatives Quillan and Crane, respectively.

Bibliography

Preface

Books

Kaufman, Herbert. *Red Tape: Its Origins, Uses, and Abuses.* Washington, D.C.: Brookings Institution, 1977.

Chapter 1

Books

Ash, Robert. *Information Theory.* New York: John Wiley & Sons, 1965.
Dunn, Edgar S., Jr. *Social Information Processing and Statistical Systems— Change and Reform.* New York: John Wiley & Sons, 1974.
Fox, Karl A. *Social Indicators and Social Theory: Elements of an Operational System.* New York: John Wiley & Sons, 1974.
King, Donald W., and Bryant, Edward C. *The Evaluation of Information Services and Products.* Washington, D.C.: Information Resources Press, 1971.
Porat, Marc Uri. *The Information Economy.* 9 vols. Stanford, Calif.: Stanford University Press, 1976.
Smith, Todd S., and Sorensen, James E. *Integrated Management Information Systems for Community Mental Health Centers.* Washington, D.C.: U.S. Government Printing Office, 1974.

Articles

Glaser, Edward. "Information Technology: Power Without Direction." *Information Technology: Some Critical Implications for Decision Makers* (1972).

Hershleifer, Jack. "Where Are We in the Theory of Information?" *American Economic Review* 63, no. 2 (1973).

Holt, Charles C. "A System of Information Centers for Research and Decision Making." *American Economic Review* 60, no. 2 (1970).

Ilchman, Warren. "The Information Revolution." *Annals of the American Academy of Political and Social Science* 412 (March 1974).

Terleckyj, Nestor E. "Measuring the Possibilities of Social Change." *Looking Ahead* (August 1970).

Other

Federal Statistics: Report of the President's Commission. 2 vols. Washington, D.C.: U.S. Government Printing Office, 1971.

Harris Survey, 1967.

Intergovernmental Task Force on Information Systems. *The Dynamics of Information Flow: Recommendations to Improve the Flow of Information Within and Among Federal, State, and Local Governments.*" Washington, D.C.: U.S. Government Printing Office, 1968.

Chapter 2

Books

Arrow, Kenneth. *The Limits of Organization.* New York: Harper and Row, 1957.

Bell, Daniel. *The Coming of Post-Industrial Society.* New York: Basic Books, 1974.

Blau, Peter. *The Dynamics of Bureaucracy.* Chicago: University of Chicago Press, 1955.

Blau, Peter, and Meyer, Marshall. *Bureaucracy in Modern Society.* New York: Random House, 1971.

Caplan, N., Morrison, A., and Stambaugh, R. J. *The Use of Social Science Knowledge in Policy Decisions at the National Level.* Ann Arbor, Mich.: Institute for Social Research, 1975.

Crozier, Michel. *The Bureaucratic Phenomenon: An Examination of Bureaucracy in Modern Organization and Its Cultural Setting in France.* Chicago: University of Chicago Press, 1964.

Downs, Anthony. *Economic Theory of Democracy.* New York: Harper and Row, 1957.

Einaudi, Luigi. *Assistance to Peru: A Case Study, 1963–8.* Santa Monica, Calif.: RAND Corporation, 1974.

Eisenstadt, S. N. *The Political System of Empires.* New York: Free Press, 1969.

Halperin, Morton H. *Bureaucratic Politics and Foreign Policy.* Washington, D.C.: Brookings Institution, 1974.

Heclo, Hugh. *A Government of Strangers.* Washington, D.C.: Brookings Institution, 1977.

Horowitz, Irving Louis. *The Rise and Fall of Project Camelot.* Cambridge, Mass.: M.I.T. Press, 1967.

Ilchman, Warren, and Uphoff, Norman. *The Political Economy of Change.* Berkeley, Calif.: University of California Press, 1971.

Levine, Robert A. *Public Planning: Failure and Redirection.* New York: Basic Books, 1972.

March, James G., and Simon, Herbert A. *Organizations.* New York: John Wiley & Sons, 1958.

Marshall, T. H. *Class, Citizenship, and Social Development.* New York: Doubleday Anchor Books, 1965.

Moynihan, Daniel P. *Coping.* New York: Random House, 1973.

———. *Maximum Feasible Misunderstanding.* New York: Free Press, 1969.

Peters, Charles, and Branch, Taylor. *Blowing the Whistle.* New York: Praeger, 1972.

Sackman, M., and Nie, Norman eds. *The Information Utility of Social Choice.* Montvale, N.J.: A.F.I.P.S. Press, 1970.

Schlesinger, Arthur. *The Imperial Presidency.* Boston: Houghton Mifflin Company, 1973.

Schultze, C. L. *The Politics and Economics of Public Spending.* Washington, D.C.: Brookings Institution, 1969.

Weber, Max. *Economy and Society.* 3 vols. Edited by Guenther Roth and Claus Wittich. New York: Bedminster Press, 1968.

Wheeler, Stanton. *On Record.* New York: Russell Sage Foundation, 1969.

Wilensky, Harold. *Organizational Intelligence.* New York: Basic Books, 1967.

Articles

Bendix, Reinhard. "Bureaucracy." *International Encyclopedia of the Social Sciences,* vol. 2. New York: Macmillan, 1970.

Campbell, Donald T. "Administrative Experiments, Institutional Records, and Non-Reactive Measures." In William Evans, ed. *Organizational Experiments.* New York: Harper and Row, 1971.

Cline, Ray S. "Policy Without Intelligence." *Foreign Policy* no. 17 (Winter 1974–75).

George, Alexander L. "The Case for Multiple Advocacy in Making Foreign Policy." *American Political Science Review* 66 (September 1972).

Gordon, Andrew et al. "Public Access to Information." *Northwestern Law Review* 68, no. 2 (May/June 1973).

Kissinger, Henry A. "Bureaucracy and Policy-Making: The Effect of Insiders and Outsiders on the Policy Process." In Morton H. Halperin and Arnold Kanter, eds. *Readings in American Foreign Policy: A Bureaucratic Perspective*. Boston: Little, Brown & Co., 1973.

Michaud, Michael A. "Communications and Controversy: Thoughts on the Future of Foreign Service Reporting." *Foreign Service Journal* (October 1968).

Walker, Jack. "Diffusion of Innovations." In Herbert Jacob and Kenneth N. Vines, eds. *Politics in the American States*. Boston: Little, Brown & Co., 1971.

Other

Campbell, Donald T. "The Experimenting Society." Address given to the American Psychological Association, September 1972.

Hauser, Phillip M. "Statistics and Politics." Paper prepared for the Annual Meetings of the American Statistical Association, August 15, 1972.

Ilchman, Warren. "Measure for Measure: Administrative Productivity in the Second Development Decade." Paper for panel seminar, March 1973.

Rose, Richard. In *Social Policies and Indicators*. New York: Social Science Research Council, 1973.

Sibley, John. "Student Says a Policeman Tried to Falsify a Report of a Holdup." *New York Times,* November 23, 1972.

Stockfish, J. A. "The Bureaucratic Pathology." In *Federal Statistics: Report of the President's Commission,* Vol. 2. Washington, D.C.: U.S. Government Printing Office, 1971.

Chapter 3

Reports and Letters

Inter-Agency Steering Committee on Uniform Corporate Reporting. Washington, D.C.: U.S. Government Printing Office, 1977.

Letter, Comptroller General Staats to Sen. Lee Metcalf, January 6, 1976.

Chapter 4

Books

Bell, Daniel. *The Coming of Post-Industrial Society*. New York: Basic Books, 1974.

Calderone, Gerald E. *Statistics About Society: The Production and Use of Federal Data.* Beverly Hills, Calif.: Sage Publications, 1974.

Caplan, N., and Barton, E. *Social Indicators '73: A Study of the Relationship Between the Power of Information and Utilization by Federal Executives.* Ann Arbor, Mich.: Institute for Social Research, 1976.

Caplan, N., Morrison, A., and Stambaugh, R. J. *The Use of Social Science Knowledge in Policy Decisions at the National Level.* Ann Arbor, Mich.: Institute for Social Research, 1975.

Horowitz, Irving Louis, ed. *The Use and Abuse of Social Science: Behavioral Science and National Policy-Making.* New Brunswick, N.J.: Transaction Books, 1971.

Sackman, M., and Nie, Norman, eds. *The Information Utility of Social Choice.* Montvale, N.J.: A.F.I.P.S. Press, 1970.

U.S., National Institute of Mental Health. *Planning for Creative Change in Mental Health Services: A Distillation of Principles on Research Utilization.* Washington, D.C.: U.S. Government Printing Office, 1971.

Use of Social Research in Federal Domestic Programs. A staff study for the Research and Technical Programs Subcommittee of the Committee on Government Operations, House of Representatives, April 1967. 3 vols. Washington, D.C.: U.S. Government Printing Office, 1967.

Weiss, Carol H. *Improving the Linkage Between Social Research and Public Policy.* New York: Columbia University Bureau of Applied Social Research, 1975.

Wildavsky, Aaron. *The Politics of the Budgetary Process.* 2d ed. Boston: Little, Brown & Co., 1974.

Articles

Havelock, Ronald. "Highway Safety Research Communications: Is There a System?" *Institute for Social Resarch, CRUSK* (March 1973).

Kitsuse, John, and Cicourel, Aaron V. "A Note on the Use of Official Statistics." *Social Problems,* no. 11 (Fall 1969).

Knorr, D. Karin. "Policymakers' Use of Social Science Knowledge: Symbolic or Instrumental?" In Carol H. Weiss, *Using Social Research in Public Policy-Making.* Lexington, Mass.: Lexington Books, 1977.

Mayer, Steven E. "Are You Ready to Accept Program Evaluation?" *P.E.R.C. Newsletter* 4, no. 1 (January/February 1975).

Roos, Noralou P. "Influencing the Health Care System: Policy Alternatives." *Public Policy* 22 (1974).

Walker, Jack. "Innovation in States Politics." In Herbert Jacob and Kenneth N. Vines, eds. *Politics in the American States.* Boston: Little, Brown & Co., 1971.

Other

Larsen, Judith. "Diffusion of Innovations Among Community Mental Health Centers." Progress report, American Institutes for Research. Palo Alto, Calif., 1973.

Lobb, Judith, and Ciarlo, James A. "Predicted Relative Utilization of Community Mental Health Centers in the City and County of Denver." Unpublished manuscript, Mental Health Systems Evaluation Project, University of Denver, 1975.

Morss, E. R., and Rich, R. F. "The Process of Specifying Information Value." Unpublished report by the Commission on Federal Paperwork, Washington, D.C., 1977.

National Academy of Sciences. *The Federal Investment in Knowledge of Social Problems.* Study project on Social Research and Development, National Research Council. Washington, D.C.: National Academy of Sciences, 1978.

Rich, R. F. "An Investigation of Information Gathering and Handling in Seven Federal Bureaucracies: A Case of the Continuous National Survey." Ph.D. dissertation, University of Chicago, 1975.

Rossman, Betty. "The Impact of Program Evaluation on Decision Making in a Community Mental Health Center." Unpublished manuscript, Mental Health Systems Evaluation Project, University of Denver, 1975.

Weiss, Carol. "Research for Policy's Sake." Address given at Case Western Reserve University, 1976.

Chapter 5

Books

Calderone, Gerald E. *Statistics About Society: The Production and Use of Federal Data.* Beverly Hills, Calif.: Sage Publications, 1974.

Chow, Gregory C. *Analysis and Control of Dynamic Economics.* New York: John Wiley & Sons, 1975.

Fishburn, Peter C. *Decision and Value Theory.* New York: John Wiley & Sons, 1964.

Marschak, Jacob. *Economic Information, Decision and Prediction: Selected Essays.* Boston and Dordrecht, Holland: Reidel Publishing Company, 1974.

Paperwork of Profits? An International Trade. National Committee on International Trade Documentation. Washington, D.C., 1971.

Peat, Marwick, Mitchell and Co. *Federal Home Loan Bank Board Burden Study.* Washington, D.C., 1977.

Pyle, Christopher. *Surveillance and Espionage in a Free Society.* Testimony presented at the Joint Hearings on Privacy of the Senate Committee on Government Operations and the Senate Judiciary Commmittee, 93rd Cong., 2d sess., June 18–20, 1974.

Sorensen, James E., and Phipps, David W. *Cost-Finding and Rate-Setting for Community Mental Health Centers.* Washington, D.C.: U.S. Government Printing Office, 1973.

State Taxation of Interstate Commerce. Report of the Special Subcommittee on State Taxation of Interstate Commerce of the Committee on the Judiciary, House of Representatives. Vol. 1. Washington, D.C.: U.S. Government Printing Office, 1964.

Thrall, R. M. et al. *Decision Processes.* New York: John Wiley & Sons, 1954.

Windle, Charles, and Bates, Peter. *Evaluation of Behavioral Programs in Community, Residential, and School Settings.* Champaign, Ill.: Research Press, 1974.

Articles

Gallagher, Cornelius. "Privacy, Human Values, and Democratic Institutions." *Computers and Automation* (October 1971).

Havelock, Ronald. "Highway Safety Research Communications: Is There a System?" *Institute for Social Research, CRUSK* (March 1973).

Lanzetta, John T., and Kanareff, Vera T. "Information Cost, Amount of Payoff, and Level of Aspiration as Determinants of Information Seeking in Decision Making." *Behavioral Sciences* F, no. 4 (1962).

McCarthy, J. "Measures of the Value of Information." *Proceedings of the National Academy of Sciences* 42, no. 9 (1956).

Payne, Aubrey H. "On Measuring the Value of Information with Implications for Communication Systems." *Institute for Naval Studies* AD 629 785 (January 1965).

Peat, Marwick, Mitchell and Co. "Small Business Reporting Burden." Paper prepared for the Office of Management and Budget. Washington, D.C., 1975.

"Project." *Michigan Law Review* 73, no. 971 (May/June 1975).

Other

Hearings Before the Commission on Federal Paperwork, June 1976 and February 1977. Letter, Maple Crude Oil Purchasing Company to the Federal Energy Administration, April 8, 1976.

Rees, Alan M., and Saracevec, Tefko. "The Measurability of Relevance." In *Technical Report, Comparative Systems Laboratory*. Cleveland, Ohio, August 1966.

Chapters 6–7

Books

Levine, Robert A. *Public Planning: Failure and Redirection*. New York: Basic Books, 1972.

Rieken, Henry W., and Boruch, Robert F. *Social Experimentation: A Method for Planning and Evaluating Social Interventions*. New York: Academic Press, 1974.

Simon, Herbert A. *Administrative Behavior*. New York: Macmillan, 1947.

Skolnick, Jerome H. *Justice Without Trial*. New York: John Wiley & Sons, 1975.

U.S., Department of Commerce. *Towards Regulatory Reasonableness*. Washington, D.C.: U.S. Government Printing Office, 1977.

Articles

Campbell, Donald T. "Administrative Experiments, Institutional Records, and Non-Reactive Measures." In William Evans, ed. *Organizational Experiments*. New York: Harper and Row, 1971.

———. "Reforms as Experiments." *American Psychologist* 24, no. 4 (April 1969).

Cohen, David K. "Politics and Research: Evaluation of Social Action Programs in Education." In Carol H. Weiss, ed. *Evaluating Action Programs*. Boston: Allyn and Bacon, 1972.

Other

Administrative Conference of the United States. "Comments Pursuant to Section 305(b) of the Railroad Revitalization and Regulatory Reform Act of 1976 on the Revised Rules of Practice Dated March 1, 1977, of the Interstate Commerce Commission with Respect to Matters Involving Common Carriers by Railroads." Mimeographed. Washington, D.C., 1977.

Campbell, Donald T. "The Experimenting Society." Address given to the American Psychological Association, September 1972.

Gilhooley, Margaret. "Preliminary Report: Evaluation of the Rule-Making Procedures for Trade Regulation Rules Under the Federal Trade Com-

mission Improvement Act." Washington, D.C., Administrative Conference of the United States, April 1975.

Ilchman, Warren. "Measure for Measure: Administrative Productivity in
the Second Development Decade." Paper for panel seminar, March
1973.

Rich, R. F. "An Investigation of Information Gathering and Handling in
Seven Federal Bureaucracies: A Case of Continuous National Survey."
Ph.D. dissertation, University of Chicago, 1975.

U.S., Congress, Senate, Committee on the Judiciary. "Report on
Regulatory Agencies to the President-Elect." 86th Cong., 2d sess.,
1960.

Chapters 8–9

Books

Cooper, E. Myles. *Guidelines for a Minimum Statistical and Accounting
System for Community Mental Health Centers.* Washington, D.C.: U.S.
Government Printing Office, 1973.

Davis, Howard R. *Planning for Creative Change in Mental Health Services:
A Manual on Research Utilization.* Washington, D.C.: U.S. Government Printing Office, 1971.

Hargreaves, W. W. et al., eds. *Community Mental Health Program Evaluation, Part I: Elements of Program Evaluation.* San Francisco: Langley-
Porter Neuropsychiatric Institute, 1974.

Isaac, Stephen, and Michael, William B. *Handbook in Research and Evaluation.* San Diego, Calif.: Robert R. Knapp, 1971.

Levine, Robert A. *Public Planning: Failure and Redirection.* New York:
Basic Books, 1972.

Redick, R. W. et al. *1970 Census Data Used to Indicate Areas with Different Potentials for Mental Health and Related Problems.* Washington,
D.C.: U.S. Government Printing Office, 1971.

VanHoudnow, Harry. *An Automated Community Mental Health Information System.* Springfield: State of Illinois Department of Mental Health,
1973.

Visotsky, Harold M., and Levy, Leo. *Manual for Evaluation of Mental
Health Programs.* Springfield: State of Illinois Department of Mental
Health, 1966.

Articles

Bloom, Bernard L. "Human Accountability in a Community Mental

Health Center: Report of an Automated System." *Community Mental Health Journal* 8 (1972).

Campbell, Donald T. "Reforms as experiments." *American Psychologist* 24, no. 4 (April 1969).

Campbell, Donald T., and Stanley, J. C. "Experimental and Quasi-Experimental Designs for Research." In N. L. Gage, ed. *Handbook of Research on Teaching.* Chicago: Rand McNally, 1963.

Ciarlo, James A., and Horrigan, Jack A. "Outcome Measurement and System Modeling for Managerial Control and Accountability." In D. Harshbarger and R. F. Maley, eds. *Behavior Analysis and Systems Analysis: An Integrative Approach to Mental Health Programs.* Kalamazoo, Mich.: Behaviordelia, 1974.

"Four Ways to Goal Attainment." *Evaluation,* Monograph 1. (Minneapolis, Minn.: Program Evaluation Project, 1973).

Kiresuk, Thomas J., and Sherman, R. E. "Goal Attainment Scaling: A General Method of Evaluating Comprehensive Community Mental Health Programs." *Community Mental Health Journal* 4 (1968).

Weiss, Carol H. "The Politicization of Evaluation Research." *Journal of Social Issues* 26, no. 4 (1970).

Other

Campbell, Donald T. "Methods for the Experimenting Society." Paper presented before the Eastern Psychological Association, April 1971.

Campbell, Donald T., and Cook, Thomas D. "The Design and Conduct of Quasi-Experiments and True Experiments in Field Settings." Unpublished manuscript, Northwestern University, 1973.

Ciarlo, James A. "Monitoring of Outcome Data: Steps Toward a System for Improving Mental Health Outcomes." Presentation at American Psychological Association Convention, Montreal, 1973.

Ciarlo, James A. et al. "How Process and Outcome Data Is Utilized by a Center's Management and Staff." Panel presentation at Annual Meeting of National Council of Community Mental Health Centers, Washington, D.C., 1975.

Hoerl, Richard. "A Manager's Use of Program Evaluation Data." Presentation at the Annual Meeting of National Council of Community Mental Health Centers, Washington, D.C., 1975.

Chapter 10

Hearings

Hearings on Privacy: The Collection, Use, and Computerization of Personal

Data, held jointly before the Senate Government Operations Ad Hoc Subcommittee on Privacy and Information Systems and the Senate Judiciary Subcommittee on Constitutional Rights, 93rd Cong., 2d sess., June 18–20, 1974.

Hearings on the Public Participation Act of 1976, Senate Judiciary Subcommittee on Administrative Practices and Procedures, 94th Cong., 2d sess., 1976.

Court Cases

International News Service v. Associated Press, 39 Sp. Ct. 68 (1918).

U.S. v. Bottone, 365 F. 2d 389 (2d Cir. 1966) cert. denied, 385 U.S. 974 (1966).

U.S. v. DiGilio, (3rd Cir. 1976) 45 *U.S. Law Week* 2002.

U.S. v. Friedman, 388 F. Supp. 963 (W.D. Pa. 1975).

U.S. v. Moriarity, 106 F. 886, 891 (N.Y. Cir. 1901).

U.S. v. Rickenbacker, 309 F. 2d 462 (2d Cir. 1962) cert. denied, 83 Sp. Ct. 542 (1963).

Books

Kaplan, Benjamin. *An Unhurried View of Copyright.* New York: Columbia University Press, 1967.

Mill, J. S. *On Liberty.* New York: Penguin Books, 1975.

Articles

Lazarus, S., and Onek, J. "The Regulators and the People." *Virginia Law Review* 57 (1971), pp. 1058–72.

Index

definition of, 148–149
efficient utilization of, 14–16,
    150–153, 155, 176–177
expenditure on, 147, 155
feedback systems in, 149, 154,
    177
and national priorities, 149–150
and role of local administrators,
    153–154, 177
Executive branch of government
and information excess, 1, 7, 25,
    38, 155
role in reducing information
    excess, 40–43, 172, 173–174

FCC. *See* Federal Communications
    Commission
FDA. *See* Food and Drug
    Administration
Federal Communications Commission
    (FCC)
clarity and coverage of standards,
    80, 86–87, 88, 112–113, 114,
    116, 119, 120
and distrust of government, 68
monitoring and enforcement of
    standards, 94, 123
procedures compared to Food and
    Drug Administration, 110
Re-regulation Task Force, 86,
    112–113
review of cases, 81, 91, 115–116,
    121, 128, 130, 134: cost of, 114
vague legislation concerning, 85,
    110–111, 112
Federal Energy Administration, 155
Federal government
citizen responsibility to, 160–162
expenditure on information, 1, 14,
    137, 139, 165–166
hidden policies of, 22
information management in, 2, 8,
    42, 139, 143–144
paperwork/information excess in,
    25, 38, 42: root causes, 4–12

See also Bureaucrats; Distrust of
    federal government; Government
    agencies; National priorities
Federal Maritime Commission
    (FMC)
clarity and coverage of standards,
    80, 87, 88, 175
monitoring and enforcement of
    standards, 14, 81, 93–94,
    135–136
public involvement in, 92–93
review and petition of cases, 14,
    80–81, 90–91, 92, 128, 130,
    131, 132, 134
vague legislation concerning,
    13–14, 80, 85, 126–127
Federal Register, 117
Federal Reports Act, 39, 170
Federal Trade Commission, 108
and intervenor compensation
    program, 164, 168
Flow of information. *See* Use of
    information, studies of
FMC. *See* Federal Maritime
    Commission
Food Additive Amendment of 1958,
    188 n.4
Food and Drug Administration
    (FDA)
clarity and coverage of standards,
    80, 85, 87, 88, 112–113, 114,
    115, 119–120
and compensation for information,
    162–163
and Delaney Amendment,
    110–111
monitoring and enforcement of
    standards, 14, 81, 94, 123–124,
    175, 188 n.4
review and petition of cases, 14,
    81, 86, 91, 118, 121, 123
Ford Foundation, 48
Foreign Service, 26
4-R Act. *See* Interstate Commerce
    Commission, and 4-R Act
Friedman case, 166, 167(table)